THE TIME AND PRICE

A study of WD Gann and the economic cycles

Peter Sutton-Smith PhD

The Time and Price
A study of WD Gann and the economic cycles

First published in Australia by Peter Sutton-Smith 2026

A catalogue record for this book is available from the National Library of Australia

ISBN: 978-0-646-73898-7 (pbk)

Cover image by: Who is Danny © (shutterstock)

Typesetting and design by Publicious Book Publishing
Published in collaboration with Publicious Book Publishing
www.publicious.com.au

For follow up information and charts please visit:
My Facebook page **The Time and Price**
Or follow on Instagram @**thetimeandprice**

Contents

Preface.. i

Introduction.. 1

Part 1: Enhancing the Technical

Sacred Numbers 13

Harmonics 17

Fibonacci Retracement and Extension 21

The Gann Fan and Price Scaling.. 31

Part 2: Discovering the Esoteric

Planetary Cycles 49

Natal Astrology 67

Putting it all Together 90

Conclusion 99

About the Author 103

Preface

Most of us conceive time as a line running from the ages, through our ancestors to us at the present moment, and extending into the unseen future.

But time is not linear. Time is circular. Time is cyclic. Time is rhythmic.

WD Gann understood this and used his knowledge of time cycles to become a legendary stock market trader. This book is written for those who wish to better understand Gann and to use his time cycle approach to track the rhythm of the economy. Using time cycles to predict the market is the real brilliance of Gann. These ideas cannot be written into the dropdown menu of a trading package. They require a deeper understanding of esoteric concepts.

Understanding the economic cycle and your current time point within the cycle are the two most important things you can ever learn. The state of the economy affects every aspect of our lives. Making the right decisions at the right time will change your life for the better.

This manuscript is not a literary masterpiece. It is written in a conversational, no nonsense style. Nevertheless, in compiling this document I have embraced the adage "to teach is to learn twice". Accordingly, I have already been rewarded by having to organize my thoughts into this paper. If the reader also gets some benefit from this knowledge, then I will be rewarded a second time.

Chapter 1
Introduction

Retirement is a major turning point in anyone's life. My retirement came with the expected mix of emotions ranging from elation to fear. But one emotion that I was not expecting was guilt. I felt (briefly) guilty because I realized that after 44 years of working as a clinical scientist in medical pathology, all my acquired knowledge and experience was never again going to be used to help someone.

That same sense of guilt has lead to the writing of this book. After 30 years of observing and trading the financial markets, I learnt the truth of the market cycles which I used to generate a significant retirement income. This book is a summary of that knowledge. This is the book I needed twenty five years ago. Hopefully documenting the lessons here in will go some way to appeasing my conscience.

In the early 1990's the Australian government legislated that all employers had to pay compulsory superannuation payments for their employees. The aim of this undertaking was to provide more money for individuals in retirement and to take the pressure of the retirement pension system. The Prime Minister at the time Paul Keating described the process as "interest upon interest upon interest". So, from this time on, every working Australian had some "skin" in the game whether they liked it or not.

By 1992 I had been working for nearly twenty years and had no thoughts of retirement or superannuation. The instigation of the compulsory superannuation scheme made me realize that my retirement was only about twenty five years away and at that point I had absolutely no retirement savings. Coincidentally, by the mid 1990's the internet was establishing itself and computer programs for charting share movements became available. I learnt to read a chart, became proficient at technical analysis and traded shares, options, option spreads, and warrants with a view to supporting myself in retirement. Whilst this type of trading is dynamic and exciting, it is also stressful and requires a significant time commitment.

Surprisingly, at the end of the day, it was my boring old superannuation that earned far more money than all my trading. Most people don't think about their superannuation. It sits at the back of their mind, unacknowledged and unloved. Its value goes up and down with the financial markets and there is no sense of control over the final outcome. But there is a way to take back control of your retirement. The secret to getting the most out of superannuation is to side step the major market downturns. The Australian superannuation system is ideally suited to this strategy because tax reconciliation is only applied when you roll your savings into an income stream at retirement. So, during the accumulation phase, it is possible to move your entire retirement savings from shares into cash without losing tax on the profits. These days this can be done simply with a click of the computer mouse. Effectively, you are selling all your shares, converting them to cash and preserving your entire account value for re-investment near the bottom of the downturn. This is a very powerful way of growing your retirement account.

In recent decades the major market downturns have been labelled "black swan events". This term is a northern hemisphere term which originates from the fact that all their swans are white and a black swan is a totally improbable and unexpected occurrence. Ironically, in southern Australia all our swans are black, so the analogy loses its meaning when translated to the southern hemisphere.

The other irony is that "black swan events" are far from improbable or unexpected. These major economic downturns are entirely predictable and have been occurring for hundreds of years. Over the last 130 years they are most easily seen documented in the movements of the share market. These regular, predictable downturns are what make viable the above superannuation strategy. These regular, rhythmic cycles are the essence of the techniques used by WD Gann.

During the 1990's I watched my retirement savings increase significantly. Using the Dow Jones Industrial index (DJI) as the world's economic barometer, this index went from about 3,000 points in 1992 to roughly 11,000 in 2000. But then from 2000 to 2002 there was a 30% decline during the "dot.com" crash and my savings reduced in proportion. Learning from this experience, in early 2008 after the market had topped out the year before, I moved my savings into cash and missed the 50% decline in the DJI during the Global Financial Crisis (GFC). The DJI went from approximately 14,000 points in 2007 to 7,000 in early 2009. Whilst not capturing the entire 50% move, I effectively retained in my account twice the value it would have had if I had stayed in the market. When re-invested in 2009, this meant that I had effectively doubled the value of any future earnings in the account. Whilst there was a certain amount of luck in the timing of this move, a few years after this I was exposed to the principles of WD Gann and discovered the real reason for these violent market movements. After ten years of market growth I again moved my money into cash in January 2020 just prior to the COVID crash, but this time I used Gann's principles of market timing. From 2009 the DJI went from 7,000 points to 29,500 in early 2020, increasing over four times in value. The COVID crash again wiped out over 30% of the Dow's value when it fell from 29,500 to 19,000 and I again retained the value in my account.

WD Gann was a legendary stock market trader who lived through the first half of the 20th century in the USA. Whilst his name gets all the glory, there many people both before and after his life time who developed "Gann" methodologies. The term "Gann" should really be a generic term for all those using time cycle analysis.

Gann's methods were unconventional. For that reason they are ridiculed and ignored by the mainstream trading/investing houses. Whilst most investment approaches concentrate on fundamental factors including price (the Y axis of a share price chart), Gann's methods also incorporate time (the X axis). He saw everything as a cycle and by knowing the time cycle of any given market, he could look back at the multiple, repeating cycles to predict and trade the future moves. This approach is encapsulated by his quote: "time is the most important factor in determining market movements and by studying the past records of the averages or individual stocks you will be able to prove to yourself that history does repeat and that by knowing the past you can tell the future".

The study of time is intriguing. What is time? What is the time right now as you read this? If you looked at a clock to gauge the hours/minutes of the day, you have simply established the current point of the Earth's daily rotation. What is the date? The date is the position of the Earth in its 365 day cycle around the sun. These are the two basic (planetary) time cycles with which we measure the progress of time on Earth. But Gann expanded on this notion and included time periods calculated from the orbital periods of the other planets. His law of vibration links the way stocks or commodities move in the financial markets to the cyclical movement of one or more planets. The beauty of this connection is that once established, it is possible to predict the future by simply extending the cycle.

Gann lived most of his life in the US. But there was a period of time when he travelled. His travels included trips through Europe, Egypt, the Middle East and India. He did this to expose himself to other cultures, to study their ancient texts and their ancient laws. He returned with an accumulative knowledge from these texts which included one significant, recurring theme. They all contained astronomical and astrological evidence of time cycles. The Ancients used this knowledge in their daily lives, but Gann, having recognized this universal truth, used it to refine his methodology for market trading.

Back in the US Gann ran a brokerage firm, became a legend in the trading arena and produced a weekly "Supply and Demand" newsletter. He also wrote several books. Most of these books are technical in nature and are now available from the internet. And many of the market practices he reveals are readily available today due to the average trader's better understanding of the markets and our better communication through computers and the internet. However, one book, The Tunnel Thru The Air (TTTTA), is one of the most contentious manuscripts ever written. In this book Gann cryptically coded most of his time cycles. The book is the story of Robert Gordon's love for Marie Stanton, and Robert's involvement in a war against the USA. This story is really a coded analogy for the bulls and bears of the share market. He cryptically documents the run up in the share market to a top in 1929 and the biggest crash in history to a bottom in 1932. The interesting thing about this book is that it was published in 1927, ***before*** these events occurred. So in it, Gann was not only documenting his cycles, but he was also using them to predict coming market events.

Many people waste years trying to de-code the time cycles in TTTTA. Some have been successful, but most are not. This book is ***not*** about looking for cycles in TTTTA. But it ***is*** about using a time cycle approach to market analysis. To this end it is worthwhile reading chapter VII of TTTTA starting on page 75 entitled "Future Cycles". In this chapter Gann lays out the background of his time cycle approach to trading.

He starts by quoting the Bible in Ecclesiastes 1:9: "The thing that hath been, it is that which shall be; and that which is done, is that which shall be done: and there is no new thing under the sun."

And again with Ecclesiastes 3:15: "That which has been is now and that which is to be hath already been."

Gann then clearly spells out his thinking on these matters with the following statements: "this makes it plain that everything works according to past cycles, and that history repeats itself in the lives of men, nations and the stock market......my calculations are based on the cycle theory and on mathematical sequences......time is the great factor that proves all things".

These few quotes encapsulate Gann's fundamental principle of time cycle repetition. There can be little doubt that his view of the markets and the world economy was based on the concept that time and events repeat themselves at set cycle lengths.

But there is one more important part to this puzzle. On page 78 he states "in order to forecast future cycles, the most important thing is to begin right, for if we have the right beginning, we will get the right ending". This quote highlights the second, critical aspect to a Gann style analysis. Gann was insistent that, as well as recognising the cycle, it is crucial to know the starting point of that cycle. In this way you have a reference point to allow identification of where you are within that cycle.

These concepts are very different to the conventional fundamental/ price based approach to market values. For this reason conventional and time based analyses are often seen as separate entities. But the X axis of any chart ***is*** time. The concept of critical time points in the movement of a market should be seen as an enhancement to conventional analysis not as something separate. The understanding of time adds the second dimension to a chart and to a market cycle.

The Ancients understood time. For millennia they documented movements in the heavens and related them to their everyday life. In the 21st century we tend to regard them as illiterate, ignorant and superstitious. With a 21st century education and 21st century industry we are overly impressed by our technology and our ability to control our environment. But even with their low tech lifestyle, the Ancients were certain of one thing. They had no doubt about cyclic nature of time and the part that the heavens played in that cycle. In the 21st century our connection with heavens has been overwhelmed by our modern lifestyle.

The principles of WD Gann involve studying time and time cycles. This endeavor requires a re-connection and a re-learning of the ancient, fundamental laws of planetary movement. Time needs to be based, not only our "normal" Earth time, but also on the movement of other planets. Incredibly, the share market is one of the few places were this connection can be observed. In studying time we are looking for ***numbers, patterns and ratios*** that continually appear in the market movements. The appearance of these "connections" and "coincidences" are not coincidental at all because they have a cyclical and a mathematical basis.

Once established, there are many ways to make use of time cycle knowledge. It is possible to short term trade a market utilising its every up and down. Or it is possible to take a long term investment approach utilising only the major market turning points. This book is concerned with the latter. In this book the principles of WD Gann will be applied to the long term economic cycles present in DJI. The US economy is the largest in the world and the DJI index has been established for nearly 130 years. The whole world watches the DJI and moves in synchronization with it. This makes the DJI the perfect barometer for the US and world's economies. This is especially pertinent because in recent decades as communication has increased via computers and the internet, the world's economies have become increasingly synchronized towards one large cycle.

Tracking the booms and busts of these large economic cycles is crucial to your financial health.

My vocation was in science and medicine. These are ***evidence*** based disciplines. If you want to prove an hypothesis, you have show the appropriate evidence. If you want to treat a disease, the treatment must be proven to be effective. In this book, with a basic understanding of Gann's time cycle principles, we will look for the numbers, the ratios and the cycles that best fit the DJI. In so doing we will find evidence of the regular economic cycles of the last 130 years. With that knowledge we will then look towards the next major market high which is due in a few years. Whilst this book is primarily concerned with the acquisition and management of retirement income, an understanding of the economic cycle is critical to all aspects of life. This is especially true if you are running a business. Knowing the timing of a market downturn gives you a chance to prepare and take the necessary action to survive the bad times.

This book is divided into two parts. The first part, "Enhancing the Technical" strives to re-establish the heavenly basis for some of our sacred numbers and then moves on to an understanding of natural harmonics. The numbers and ratios derived from these analyses are then used with two indicators which are included in every share trading program. The Fibonacci retracement/extension tool is used to predict ***price*** points for the market tops and bottoms. The Gann Fan, in conjunction with lessons from Gann's famous "Coffee Letter", is used to predict ***time*** points for the market tops and bottoms. The use of these two indicators will not be much of a "jump" for most people familiar with market trading, but they do provide remarkably accurate time/price points in the market.

The second part of the book, "Discovering the Esoteric" may be a challenge for some readers. In this section we will enter Gann's esoteric world and look at the major time points using two key time cycles. “Planetary Cycles” covers the major cycle that has governed the timing of the ups and downs of the world economies for more than one hundred years. Whilst, “Natal Astrology” focuses only on the DJI and a cycle of particular planets used to predict the share market’s highs and lows. These two cycles are very closely related, but they are not the same.

Before we start this journey you should know that a basic level of knowledge is assumed in the reading of this book.

The use of a computer and, in particular, the use of charting software (including indicators) is an important pre-requisite. Fortunately, these days there is no need to purchase a computer package or share price data. The free online version of **TradingView** is used for all share price charting in this book.

The reader will need a basic understanding of astronomy including the Earth’s titled axis, the Earth’s plane of orbit, the solar system and the planet’s revolution times.

A basic understanding of astrology is also necessary, including the 12 signs of the zodiac and the concept of both heliocentric and geocentric planetary perspectives. To aid the reader, the free download of **Astrolog** is used for all astrological charting.

Part 1

Enhancing the Technical

Chapter 2
Sacred Numbers

To commence our journey into Gann, we will look at a few of the basic numbers which are used throughout this book and highlight their heavenly connections. In so doing we will see that, even in the modern world, our everyday lives are still connected to movements in the heavens as they have been for millennia. The topic of sacred numbers is a huge subject and accordingly there is plenty to be found on the internet for those who wish to pursue a more detailed investigation.

Number Three

The earth's rotational axis is tilted at 23.4° to the plane of the earth's orbit. So as we revolve around the sun during the year we get the four seasons: summer, autumn, winter, spring. From our perspective on earth, the sun moves north of the equator to 23.4° north latitude in June for the northern hemisphere summer, and then travels back to 23.4° south of the equator in December for the southern hemisphere summer. These extreme movements of the sun in June and December are the solstices, and if you look at an astrological chart you will see that these dates correspond to the sun moving into the houses of Cancer and Capricorn respectively. Hence we have a geographical/astrological connection with the Tropic of Cancer and the Tropic of Capricorn which define the "tropics" on the globe of the earth.

But the most important aspect of the solstice is that the sun stands still. Because of the earth's titled axis the sun is always moving. Climbing higher in the sky for the longer days of summer and lower in the sky for the shortened days of winter. In addition, the points of sunrise and sunset move along the horizon, northwards for the northern hemisphere summer and southwards for winter. But there are ***three*** days at each solstice where the sun stops moving as it reverses its direction into the new season. The word solstice comes from two Latin words: sol = sun and stice = stopped.

Ancient cultures understood the cyclic nature of the seasons, but without our knowledge of the solar system they had no understanding of the cause of the sun's movement. They built temples to monitor the sun's movements. The Celts are thought to have built Stonehenge which is aligned with the summer and winter solstices. These ***three*** day time periods were sacred to them, especially the winter solstice. In the middle of a bitter English winter, they needed to observe and celebrate the reversal of the sun's southward movement. The returning of the sun signified the repeating of the cycle, bringing with it the promise of warmer and more fruitful times.

Number Seven

Have you ever wondered why there are seven days in a week? The days of the week are named after the seven visible deities in the sky. The seven visible heavenly bodies that move amongst the fixed stars: the Sun, the Moon, and the planets Mercury, Venus, Mars, Jupiter and Saturn. In modern English we have lost this connection, but if you look at the Latin or French names for the days of the week, the relationship is obvious.

English	Latin	French	Planet
Sunday	deis Solas	Dimanche	Sun
Monday	deis Lunae	Lundi	Moon
Tuesday	deis Martis	Mardi	Mars
Wednesday	deis Mercurii	Mercredi	Mercury
Thursday	deis Jovis	Jeudi	Jupiter
Friday	deis Veneris	Vendredi	Venus
Saturday	deis Saturni	Samedi	Saturn

Source: Internet and PSS

It is possible to see Uranus with the naked eye, but the conditions have to be perfect and you need to know where to look. The Ancients did not see it or document its movement. If they had, we may well have an eight day week.

The number seven and septimal law dates back to Mesopotamia with multiple creation stories, good luck, bad luck and musical scales all connected to this number.

Number Twelve

The orbital period of Jupiter is 12 years. Jupiter is the largest planet in the solar system. Its mass is greater than all the other planet's combined. It is the brightest "star" in the night sky (once Venus has set).

The number twelve is everywhere in our lives and has been for centuries. There were 12 tribes of Israel, Jesus had 12 disciples, there are 12 signs in the Zodiac, there are 12 months in a year, our daily (hourly) time is measured in lots of 12 (24), in the first millennium Charlemagne's monetary system used a base 12 system, more recently some pre-decimal currencies still used base 12 (e.g. 12 pence in a shilling), there are 12 inches in a foot and we still use a dozen as a measure of quantity.

Number Thirty

Saturn is the second largest planet in the solar system and its orbital period is 30 years. The number thirty occurs commonly in our lives and in the work of Gann. There are roughly 30 days in a month. This 30 day period corresponds to a one degree movement of Saturn. We use these monthly increments as a sub-division of the yearly Earth cycle. The Zodiac is similarly sub-divided with each house occupying 30 degrees. The ***thirty*** degree increment of a cycle was an important, fundamental unit for Gann.

Three Hundred and Sixty

360 is the number of degrees in a circle (cycle). The orbital period of the Earth (365 days) is very close to ***three hundred and sixty***. And "coincidentally" the product of the orbital periods of Jupiter and Saturn (12 x 30) is ***360***.

This chapter briefly introduces a few basic numbers which we will use in later discussions. We use these numbers every day in our busy lives without considering their heavenly connections. Acknowledging the origins of these numbers is the first step to re-connecting with the heavens and the first step down the road to understanding the esoteric concepts used by Gann.

Chapter 3
Harmonics

Everything has a vibration. You and I have a vibration. Everything around us vibrates. The share market vibrates. Gann understood this and he claimed that collective behaviour created cycles. His first rule of trading was to trade only active markets. He reasoned that the share market was one of the most exquisite examples of "collective behaviour", and as such, the repeating patterns could be used to predict where the general market was heading. He called this his "Law of Vibration".

We can demonstrate some of the key points of this concept using the harmonics of a vibrating string (Figure 1).

Gann's harmonics are based around the natural harmonic ratio of 2:1, ***two*** waveforms with ***one*** node. So in the 1st, 2nd, 4th and 8th harmonics we can see a simple doubling of the waveforms with each step. The 1, 2, 4, 8 lines are common to many of the Gann tools in various charting packages.

In contrast, Pythagoras saw everything as groups of ***three***. He is the triangle guy we all learnt about in school and he lived around 500BC. It is claimed by some that his "sum of the squares" theorem was well known in the ancient world and that he learnt of it during his many travels. Nevertheless the theorem still bears his name and his harmonics are based on the ratio 3:2.

In Figure 1, the 3rd harmonic represents an example of Pythagorean harmonics with a ***three*** waveform pattern and ***two*** nodes. Note that the positions of these 3rd harmonic nodes do not appear to fit with doubling nodes of the 2nd, 4th and 8th harmonics.

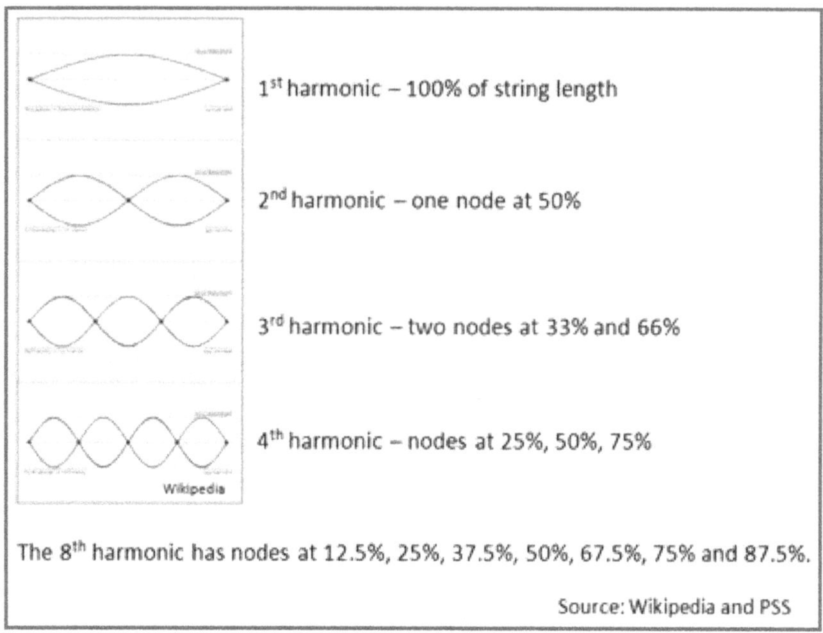

Figure 1. The harmonics of a single string.

But this is not the case. To prove it let us move a little further into musical theory noting the connection to some of our sacred numbers. The 8th harmonic divides the string into eight parts and there are eight notes in an octave, right? Wrong. There are actually only ***seven*** notes (and seven steps) in an octave with the eighth note being a repeat of the first note and the start of the next octave.

Any octave scale is made up of ***seven*** notes comprising of both whole tones and semi-tones. But if we count all the possible semi-tones, we find there are ***twelve*** semi-tones in an octave.

Figure 2 is a representation of the generic octave scale using "Do, Re, Mi…" etc. Let us assume that the first "Do" has a frequency of

1 and the second "Do", which is an octave higher, has a frequency of 2. If we now fill in the natural frequencies for each note in the scale, the numbers should look familiar to you. The frequency of the notes correspond to nodal positions in the harmonics above. Even the "out of step" Pythagorean nodes fit perfectly into the octave scale. Re is 1/8th of the way to the next Do and is the first node of the 8th harmonic. Mi is the first node of the 4th harmonic. Fa is the first node of the 3rd harmonic. So is the node of the 2nd harmonic. La is the second node of the 3rd harmonic. And Ti is the last node of the 8th harmonic.

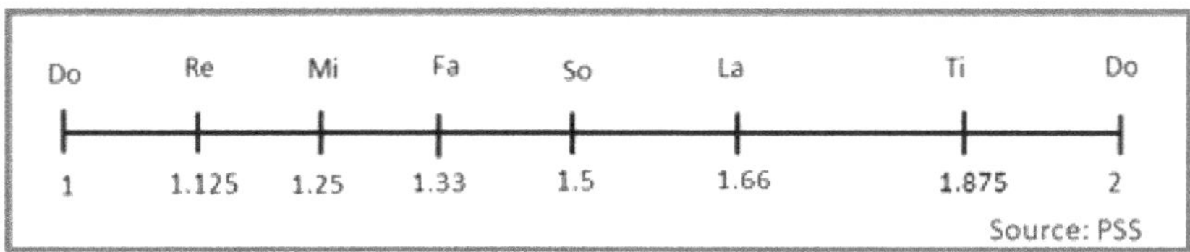

Figure 2. The generic octave scale.

These same harmonic numbers can also be seen in the Gann symbol in Figure 3. A circle, representing the 360° cycle, contains a square and a triangle. The square symbolizes the cardinal cross (4 points at 90° angles) of the 4th harmonic with points at 0°, 90°, 180° and 270°. The triangle (or trine with ***three*** points at 120° angles) embodies the third harmonic with points at 0°, 120° and 240°.

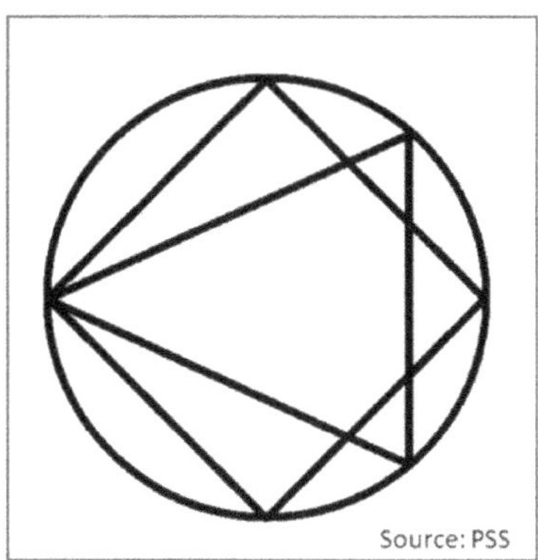

Figure 3. The Gann symbol.

These mathematical connections keep occurring when studying the tools that Gann used for share market analysis. Sacred numbers are relevant in the study of harmonics and music. These same harmonic numbers then become relevant in the study of price movements.

Chapter 4

Fibonacci Retracement and Extension

Fibonacci

Fibonacci was a mathematician who lived in the 13th century. He is credited with bringing the decimal, Indo-Arabic numeral system to Europe. But today in the world of the share market, he is perhaps most famous for his number sequence in which each number is the sum of the previous two. This sequence is:

1 1 2 3 5 8 13 21 34 55 89 144 232 377 610 987 1597 ....

The interesting thing about this sequence is that (apart from the first few numbers) the average ratio of one number to the next is 1.618. This number is known as Phi (Ø) and is generally regarded as the divine or golden ratio. Fibonacci numbers and the golden ratio can be seen in nature with the petal numbers in flowers, the arrangement of leaves on a stem, and the spiral of shells. The human body also reflects this ratio with "beauty" seen as having body and/or facial features in this proportion.

But the golden ratio is not just a physical ratio. Interestingly, it is also a ***time*** ratio. And here we find yet another mathematical link to the heavens. Venus is Earth's sister planet which is similar in size and density to Earth, but too close to the sun for life. Venus revolves around the sun every 225 days. If we divide 225 into the Earth's 365 days we once again get 1.62, the golden ratio.

Other numbers can also be derived from the Fibonacci sequence. If you divide any number by the number two positions ahead of it in the sequence, you get 0.38. A number divided by the number three positions ahead equals 0.24. Dividing by a number two positions below gives 2.62, and dividing by number three positions below gets 4.24.

These are the default percentages of the Fibonacci retracement tool in most charting packages.

0% 23.6% 38.2% 50% 61.8% 100% 161.8% 261.8% 423.6%

If we again look at the ***time*** ratios using the revolution times of the four inner planets, we get some remarkably similar numbers.

Mercury (88 days)/Earth (365 days) = 24%

Mercury (88 days)/Venus (225 days) = 39%

Earth (365 days)/Mars (687 days) = 53%

Venus (225 days)/Earth (365 days) = 62%

These numbers demonstrate yet another cosmic "coincidence" linking the heavens with the everyday world of share market trading.

Using the Fibonacci retracements/Extensions

If you have played around with any stock charting software you will be aware of the large number of charting tools available to augment the graphic price data. The Fibonacci retracement/ extension tool is one of these tools and it so widely used that it is built into all charting packages, even the free ones. Although the standard Fibonacci percentage settings are usually the default values seen above, virtually all charting packages will allow you to change these percentages. This opens up the use of other retracement levels.

The Dow Jones Index is a large and active market which fulfills Gann's main criteria for trading. The DJI also lends itself well to the use of the Fibonacci retracements/extensions.

Price Retracements

Using the Fibonacci tool to estimate price retracements is relatively straight forward. Simply stretch the tool graphic between the bottom and the top of the price movement of interest and read the potential retracement levels. The default percentage retracement levels will probably be 23.6%, 38.2%, 50%, 61.8% and 100% as discussed above. I tend to use the tool "upside down" with the 0% at the top and the 100% at the bottom. In this way you can read off the percentage of the upward movement to which the price has retraced. If you wish, you can add in the 76.4% level, which is only the mirror image of the 23.6% level (i.e. 76.4% is simply 23.6% back from 100%). To my mind, the 23.6%, 50% and 76.4% levels are essentially the ratios seen in the 4th harmonic above. And the 38.2% and 61.8% are similar to the 3th harmonic 33% and 66% levels. So whilst I have these five harmonic levels in my mind, I rarely go to the trouble of changing from the default Fibonacci levels.

Figure 4 shows an example of how to use this retracement tool. The last major cycle took place from the bottom in 1987 to a top in 2007. Placing the 0% line at the top of the market in 2007 and dragging the 100% to the bottom in 1987 will display the default retracement levels. The GFC crash of 2008-09 can be seen as a retracement back to the 62% level. Note how the other levels line up roughly with peaks and troughs in the years preceding the final high.

Figure 4. The DJI 1987-2009 with the retracement levels overlaid.

Figure 5 shows the run up from 1987 to the dot.com high of 2000. When the retracement tool is applied to this period it can be seen that the retracement of 2003 is about the 38% level. In this case the alignment is not perfect, but the other retracement levels do correspond to other features in the chart, indicating that this is the best fit for this charted period.

Figure 5. The DJI 1987-2003 with the retracement levels overlaid.

Figure 6 shows the 11 year period at the beginning of the current cycle. Using the price gain from the bottom in 2009 to the 2020 peak, the COVID19 crash this time represented a 50% retracement. This level of about 18,000 can be seen as a significant resistance/ support level with several price rejections throughout 2015 and 2016, a final breakout through in the middle of 2016 and then a small retracement back to this level before the market moved on. Note again the other levels and the market reaction around these levels reinforcing the significance of these retracement percentages.

Figure 6. The DJI 2009-2020 with the retracement levels overlaid.

If you are new to charting, the Fibonacci retracement tool is easy to use and you will soon get proficient with it. We will re-visit price retracements in later chapters.

Price Extensions

Using the Fibonacci extensions is a little more complex than the retracements. For plotting the extensions the Fibonacci tool is used up the "right way" with the 100% line at the top of the retracement and the 0% line at the bottom. The extensions are then used to try and pick the top of the market. The application of the extension tool is valid over any time frame, but the calculation of the extensions is most accurate over longer periods including the major cycles.

There are two aspects to using the extensions efficiently.

1. Knowing where to draw the 100-0% levels.
2. Knowing which percentages to use as the extension levels.

100-0% levels

Some aspects of using these charting extensions are more art than science. The science is in the mathematics of the extension levels. The art is knowing where to draw them. Now remember, we are not trying to predict a market top a few weeks or months from the previous bottom. We usually are working up these extension levels towards the end of the upwards price run because we know ***when*** the top is due (see later).

In any trending market there are inevitable retracements. But all retracements are not equal. Simple, short retracements are common and the upward market trend usually resumes quickly after this brief interruption. But there are other retracement periods that are not so simple. A new market high is not made after a retracement and there is either a period of sideways movement or a brief down trend before the main upward trend resumes. These ***significant*** retracement periods are the areas of interest.

The second half of the 1987-2007 cycle is shown in Figure 7. The dot.com bust from 2000-2003 can be seen clearly. But during the recovery from the 2003 low there are also two more periods where the market goes into a down trend or trades sideways before the top in 2007. These three periods are examples of significant retracements which can be used for drawing the 100-0% levels.

Similarly, in Figure 8 the first half of the current cycle is shown with the market topping out in early 2020 before the COVID19 crash. The GFC crash of 2007-2009 can be seen along with three other periods when the market goes into a down trend during the larger up trend from 2009-2020.

Figure 7. The DJI showing significant retracements between 2000-2007.

Figure 8. The DJI showing significant retracements between 2007-2020.

Extension Percentages

In forecasting extension levels for the DJI, we do not use the default Fibonacci extension levels. The 162% level does work to a degree for shorter time periods, but for the longer cycles there are better percentages. A combination of both the Pythagorean (X3) multiples and the Gann (X2) multiples have proved to be most effective.

The Pythagorean levels are: 150% (3 X 50%), 300%, 600%.

The Gann levels are: 200%, 400%, 800%.

So the Fibonacci extension tool should be set to 0%, 50%, 100%, 150%, 200%, 300%, 400%, 600% and 800%. Occasionally the market may require additional levels.

The 100-0% lines are drawn from the top to the bottom of the ***significant*** retracements. The extensions derived from the largest retracement normally prove to be the most accurate in predicting the market top. The smaller retracement extensions are used to provide reinforcement for one or more of these larger levels, thus narrowing down the number of possibilities for the top of the trend.

Figure 9 again shows the last half of the 1987-2007 cycle, now with the extensions drawn using the relevant retracements. You can see that the major retracement from 2000-2003 defines the top of the market in 2007 using the Pythagorean 150% extension. The two smaller retracements reinforce the significance of this level with the close alignment of the 400% extension levels in both cases. The alignment of these three extension levels can be used to produce a potential price zone for the market top (light green).

These alignments demonstrate the meaning behind Gann's quote "my calculations are based on the cycle theory and on mathematical sequences". The depth of each of these retracements is related to the larger market movement, but they can be related in different ways. The extension percentages derived from each retracement are often not the same (in this case two are the same), but when ***combined*** on the chart the ***hidden, future price*** point is revealed.

Figure 10 shows the first half of the current cycle from 2009 with the extensions drawn from each significant retracement. Again, the large retracement of the GFC from 2007-2009 is the critical feature. The 300% extension defines the market top in 2020 and this level (and only this level) is reinforced by close alignment of extensions

Figure 9. The combined price extensions
define the market top in 2007.

Figure 10. The combined price extensions
define the market top in 2020.

based on all three other retracements. The green price zone is drawn using the combination of all four extensions. And again, they show the mathematical relationship between each retracement and the market top.

It should be noted that the 150% extension from the 2007-2009 retracement is also reinforced by the 2011, 300% extension. This 18,000 point alignment is a legitimate price level which eventually becomes a resistance/support level for the 2015-16 highs and then the 2020 retracement (Figure 6). Despite this alignment, when the market reaches this point in 2015-16 it was not mistaken for a market top. Using our time cycle knowledge, we knew that the ***mid-cycle high was not due until about 2019*** (see later). We had to "sit tight" and wait to see what the market would reveal. Ultimately there were two more retracements which helped define the true market high.

In this chapter we have taken one of the most widely used chart drawing tools, the Fibonacci retracement/extension tool, and re-calibrated it with ratios derived from Gann and Pythagorean harmonics. This enhancement is particularly suited to the DJI. Using the combined extension levels allows very close price estimation for the top of the market, but it does not tell you ***when*** this level is going to be reached. To accomplish this we need to enter Gann's esoteric world of time cycles, but before we do that, there is one other technical drawing tool which does allow the time component of the market to be added into the analysis. This drawing tool, like the Fibonacci tool, also requires augmentation by factors derived from the work of WD Gann.

Chapter 5

The Gann Fan and Price Scaling

The Gann Fan

The Gann fan is another technical drawing tool which is included in all charting software. This tool is less used and less understood that the Fibonacci retracement tool. Nevertheless, when calibrated correctly the Gann fan can be used to decipher time/price information from historic market movements and it can be used to find both market tops and market bottoms.

The fan bears Gann's name due to the arrangement and proportion of the fan lines. The numbers should look familiar to you as they are the waveforms seen in the harmonics from chapter 3. Figure 11 shows a standard Gann fan (red lines) with blue squares superimposed to explain the derivation of the Gann lines. It can be seen that the 1/1 line runs at a 45° angle across the diagonal of the bottom left square. The steeper 1/2, 1/3, 1/4 lines run from the same point of origin at the bottom left, through the top right corners of the series of squares that are stacked on top of each other. Similarly, the shallower 2/1, 3/1, 4/1 lines run from the point of origin through the top right corners of a series of squares stacked side by side. When using this tool in a charting program, the point of origin is normally placed at a low and the 1/1 line dragged to the desired position with the other lines following in proportion.

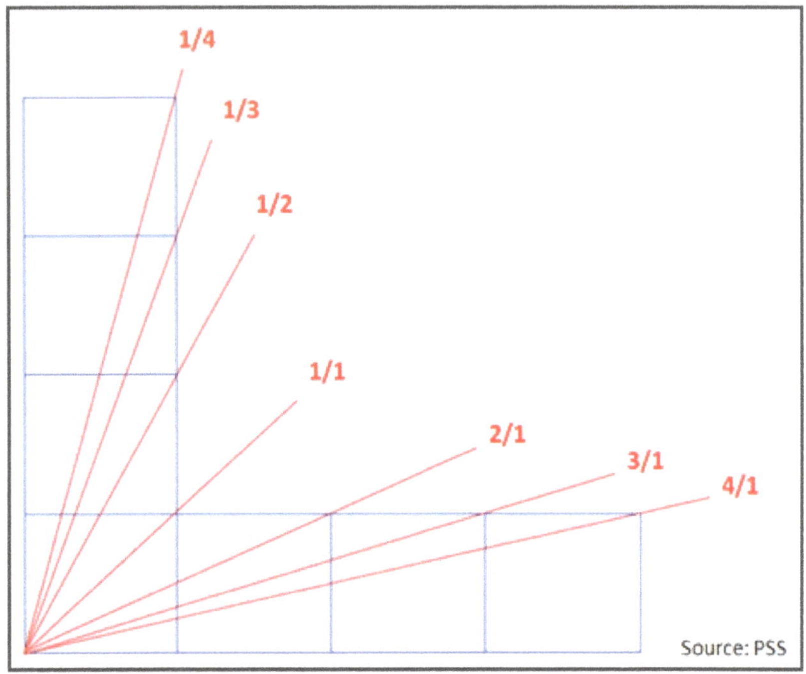

Figure 11. The Gann fan.

The Coffee Letter

Gann ran an advisory service with newsletters for his subscribers. He made these subscribers sign an agreement to not pass on or reveal his methodologies which were detailed in these newsletters. For this reason there is very little of his work available in the public domain. The famous "coffee letter", which he wrote in 1954, is one exception to this.

There is much conjecture over Gann's use of the planets for timing the market. For the most part, his work has been ridiculed and ignored by main-stream market traders who cannot rationalize the connection between planetary movement and the financial markets. This may be because Gann uses the words "cause" and "effect" when explaining his law of vibration and his concept of time cycles. I also have doubts over a "cause and effect" relationship between a market and a heavenly body. But I can conceive that the specific vibration (behaviour) of a market could be in synchronization with the vibration of a (heavenly) time cycle. This concept is similar to the notion of the "energy spectrum" in quantum physics which states that particles can only have certain energy levels which are based on the particle's wave (vibrational) behaviour. And so to progress this thought further, the specific vibrational energy of a market can conceivably be the same as the vibration of a heavenly body.

No matter what you believe, one look at the first two pages of the coffee letter (readily available on the internet) should dispel any doubts about Gann's use of the heavens in his market analysis. This letter talks about the coffee price in relation to angles, movements and revolutions of the various planets. And uses both heliocentric (sun centric) and geocentric (earth centric) aspects of these planets. There is an enormous amount of information in this one newsletter if you know what to look for. I cannot imagine how much knowledge his subscribers would have accumulated over the years if the content of this one letter is anything to go by. It is no wonder that Gann did not want this knowledge randomly distributed throughout the trading community.

Figure 12 shows a reproduction of the first page of the letter and we will now use some of the embedded knowledge to augment the use of the Gann fan.

Market Tops

Scaling the Price

One of Gann's basic principles was that major turning points in the market occurred when time and price "squared out". He believed that time and price were the same thing, so that a market top (for example) would occur in the future when the time elapsed

MAY COFFEE SANTOS D
March 19, 1954
High 8729

Using a scale of one point to one degree, 8729 equals 29° Gemini.
Using a scale of 30 points to one degree, equals 21° Capricorn.
Using the Jupiter scale of 12 points to one degree, equals 7° 30' Aries.
Using one cent to one degree, equals 27° 16' Gemini.

The dollar value is $26,171.00, which equals 11° 45' Capricorn.
The average price of 5 options on March 19, 1954 was 8663 which equals 28° Aries, or 60° from Heliocentric Jupiter. Heliocentric Jupiter is 20° 35' Gemini, which means that the price of 8729 was at this degree.
Heliocentric Uranus is 21° 52' Cancer and the price at 21° Capricorn is opposite to this.

April 16, 1954 is 276 months from April 16, 1931, low 435. Using 50 points per month, the 45° angle crossed 8715 on March 19, 1954, and the Sun has moved 8253 degrees from April 16, 1931. Add this to 435 gives 8688 as the resistance angle.

MARCH COFFEE - October 1, 1936 low 300. Time to April 1, 1954 210 months at 30 points per month, the 45° angle crosses at 5600, and at 40 points per month, it crosses at 8700.

1931, April 16 to March 19, 1954 - Geocentric Saturn moved 285° 38'. This would give a price of 8572. 1936, October 1 to March 19, 1954 - Geocentric Saturn moved 231°, which would equal a price of 7230.

1940, May 15 to March 19, 1954 - Saturn moved 181° 35', which gives a price of 6990 and using 45 points to one degree would give 8715.

1940, August 19 - Saturn moved 173° 23'. At 45 points to one degree, this equals 8760 price.

Source: Internet and PSS

Figure 12. Page 1 of the coffee letter.

was equal to the increase in the price. Now this alignment is conceivable when the market has a value of only a few hundred points, as the DJI did in the early 1900's. But at the time of writing the Dow is over 30,000 and this higher value makes a 1:1, time:price relationship almost impossible. Even in 1954 Gann appears to be having the same issue with the coffee price. In 1954 coffee was at 8729 and Gann was talking about scaling the price in different ways to allow for this larger number. In the first paragraph of the coffee letter (Figure 12), we can see mentioned two of our sacred numbers ***twelve*** (Jupiter) and ***thirty*** (Saturn) which he used as multiples of price per zodiac degree (day). Further to this, in the following paragraphs he continues to use various scaling factors to estimate price including points per month and points per degree of planetary movement.

Noting these various scaling factors, I decided to carry out my own investigation into price scaling using the run up in the DJI to the 2020 market top before the COVID crash. I analysed this very rapid gain in the index from the bottom of the last significant retracement (Figure 6) on 26/12/2018 to the top of the market on 12/02/2020. I wanted the market to show me the scaling that was appropriate to today's prices. I listed the degrees travelled by each planet and each pair of planets (synodic cycles) over the 14 month time period and divided these degrees into the price increase over the same period. I was looking for numbers that jumped out at me such as sacred numbers, astronomical/astrological numbers, or significant fractions of these numbers. My original scribblings are seen in Figure 13.

You can see that this investigation did indeed produce some significant numbers circled in the points/degree column. You can see numbers including 11.9 (the orbital period of Jupiter), 236 (close to 240°/double trine), 357 (close to 360°), 15.78 (half the orbital period of Saturn), 29 (close to one Saturn year). Converting these numbers to Earth time allows us to use these scaling factors

DJI 2018 L → 2020 H

365+5+31+12 = 413 days

26/12/18 21712 12/2/20 29568 = 7856 pts

Helio				pts/degree
E	95	143	408°	19.25
S	275	323	408°	
Moon	95	143	408°	
Mer	210	83	233+4×360 = 1673°	4.70
V	132	73	661°	11.9
Mar	38.86	235.49	197° 196.63	39.8
J	246.36	279.61	33.25°	236.3
S	281.35	293.82	12.47°	630
U	31	35	4°	1,964
node	117	95	-22°	357.1

E/V 1069°
M/E 605°
M/V 858°
J/M 230°
J/S 45°

Geo				
E	95	143	408	19.25
S	275	323	408	
Moon	155	197	360+42 = 402°	19.54
Mer	256	341	360+85 = 445°	17.65
V	228	6	360+132+6 = 498°	15.78
Mar	356	267	271° m retro	29.0
J	250	286	36° retro -10 ⇒ 56°	218.2 while retro 14[illegible]
S	280	296	16° retro -7 ⇒ 30°	491 26[illegible]
U	28	31	3°	2618.7
node	117	95	-22°	357.1

Source: PSS

Figure 13. My original notes on planetary movement of the DJI 2018-2020.

on a normal, daily price chart. This is accomplished by multiplying the points/degree X 365/the orbital period of the particular planet (e.g. for Venus above = 11.9 X 365/225). Doing this with the above five numbers results in a range of numbers from 19.25 to 19.9 points per degree. You can see that the movement of the Sun/ Earth in the above investigation came in at the bottom end of this number range.

The orbital period of Saturn is 29.5 years which is normally rounded up to 30 years. Applying the highly significant Pythagorean ratio of

66% (0.66 or 2/3's) to 29.5 results in the number of 19.5, which is right in the middle of the above range for points moved per degree (day). As a result of this, it appears that all the planets mentioned in this study show, in one way or another, a connection to the number 30. "The Saturn scale" as mentioned in the second line of the first paragraph of the coffee letter.

Scaling the Fan

The Gann fan is drawn from a major market low ***using the selected scaling***. Setting the 1/1 line is crucial when using this tool. The results from the above investigation suggest that a 30/1 scaling should be used for the 1/1 line. To do this, go forward one year (365 days or 360° degrees of planetary movement) from the selected low, draw a vertical reference line and ensure the 1/1 line intersects 10,800 points higher than the value of the low. This number is derived from 360° X 30 points/degree = 10,800 points and gives the 1/1 line an actual slope of 30/1 (Figure 14).

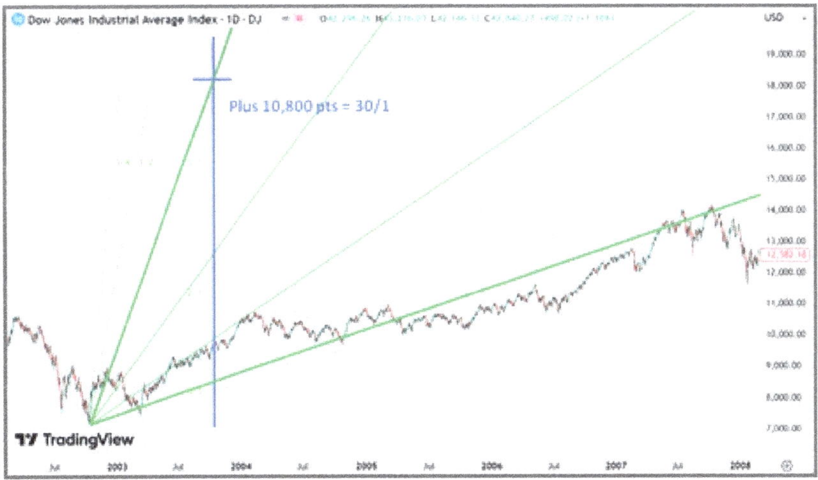

Figure 14. The 30/1 Gann fan drawn from 2002 low.

Drawing the standard Gann fan on the chart with the 1/1 line at a slope of 30/1 (30 points per day) will allow you to see which segment of the fan is relevant to the market period being analysed. In Figure 14 the fan is drawn from the low in 2002 with a view to identifying the market top in 2007. It can be seen that the market movement over those five years is largely defined by the 4/1 – 8/1 lines. Note that both the 1/3 and 3/1 lines have been removed.

Once drawn, the Gann fan can be used in either of two ways to estimate the time/price of a market top. If the time point of the top is known, the various fan lines can be used to estimate the price on that date. This is what Gann was doing in the coffee letter in 1954. He already knew the time of the market high and was trying to estimate the coffee ***price***.

If the price of the market top is known, the fan lines can give ***time*** estimates for the market to reach this point. In the above 2002–2007 market example, the Fibonacci extension alignments from the previous chapter have provided a reasonable estimate of the price zone at the top of the market (Figure 9). If we now add this price level to the fan, you can see that the combination of the price zone and the 8/1 line provides a reasonable estimate of the ***time*** and ***price*** point at the market top in 2007 (Figure 15).

Figure 15. The Fibonacci price zone and the scaled Gann fan combined for the market top.

However, it is possible to go one step further. This initial time/price point can be reinforced by creating similar, scaled fans from other significant market bottoms. These market retracements include the market lows we used to reinforce the Fibonacci price extensions in chapter 4. If you re-read paragraphs 3-7 of the coffee letter you will see that Gann was also doing something similar using the market lows of 1931, 1936 and 1940 to estimate the coffee price in 1954.

Using the 8/1 line from the 2002 low as a reference, Figure 16 shows the addition of three similarly scaled fans originating from other retracement lows. Some of the lines have been removed for clarity. You can see that the coincidence of lines from each fan with the expected price zone, aligns well with the top of the market in October 2007. Note that the slopes of the lines are not the same in each fan. The earlier retracements, including the 2002 low, define the market top with the shallow 8/1 lines, whilst the two more recent retracements align with the top using the steeper 4/1 lines. The black ellipse is draw to include the intersection of all four lines with the price zone.

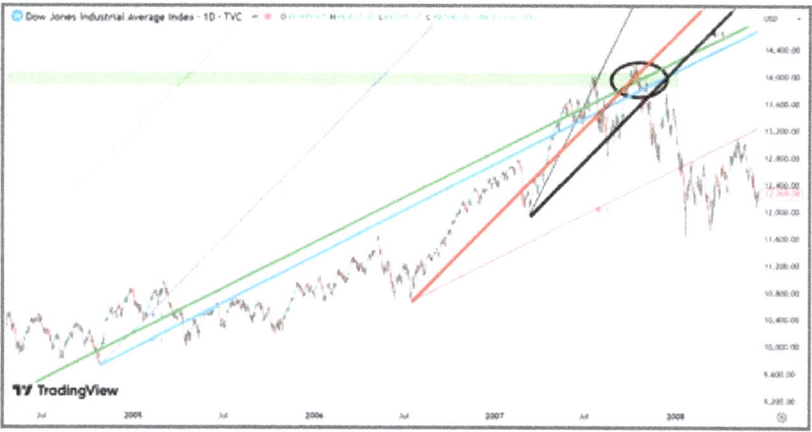

Figure 16. Additional fans show lines coincident with the market top.

The 2007 market high is a very convenient example of the scaled Gann fans because the default fan lines are all that are required to show the timing of the top. However, this is not always the case because longer time periods from market bottom to proposed market top result in more divergent lines. This divergence is most noticeable from a major market bottom to the mid-cycle correction (see later). This time period can be over ten years with the recent 2020 (COVID) crash being nearly eleven years from the 2009 low. Figure 17 shows the scaled Gann fan over this time period. You can see how well the 4/1 – 8/1 sector defines the market movement over this time and you can also see that none of the default lines define the top of the market in 2020. So in this situation, this tool needs to be enhanced.

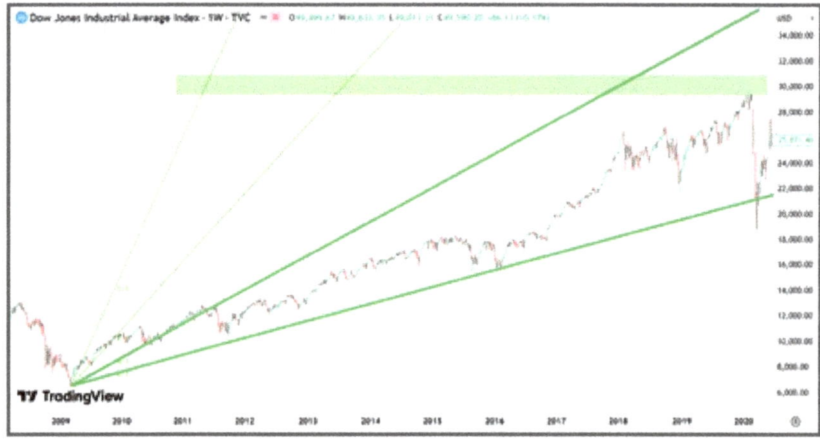

Figure 17. The scaled Gann fan from 2009 to 2020.

To address this problem we need to re-focus on the coffee letter. Analysis of the third to seventh paragraphs of the coffee letter reveals how Gann approached this issue. In these paragraphs he talks about scaling the coffee price at 50, 30, 40 and 45 points per month or degree of Saturn's movement (each degree movement of Saturn is a month). So if we assume a month has 30 days, then the 30 points per month scaling is really the same as the 1/1 fan line. Forty five points a month equates to a 1.5/1 line, and 50 and 40 points per month equate to 1.66/1 and 1.33/1 lines respectively. So once again we find the 50%, 66% and 33% harmonic ratios continuing to appear in Gann's work, reinforcing their importance in analysing market movements. In this case we are using these numbers to augment the slope of the fan lines.

So to follow Gann's lead, these extra lines can be added to the relevant sector of the fan to counter the divergence of the lines over time. However, the lesser used Gann fan tool does not allow additional input for the line values like the Fibonacci tool, so they must be added manually. This can be achieved simply by using the Fibonacci retracement tool set to 0.66, 0.5 and 0.33. Figure 18 shows this sub-division added into the 4/1 – 8/1 sector of the fan in Figure 17.

Sub-dividing this sector with the additional three lines shows a close correlation between the market high and the added 66% line (Figure 18). This line suggested the market top would be in late 2019 which is pretty close to the actual top. Analysing the other fan lines reveals that the standard 4/1 line suggested an early 2018 top, and the added 50% line suggested a late 2020 top. So you can see that although we have sub-divided this sector, the extra lines still intersect the price zone at time points which are well spaced, so there can be no ambiguity about the timing of the market top/price zone intersection.

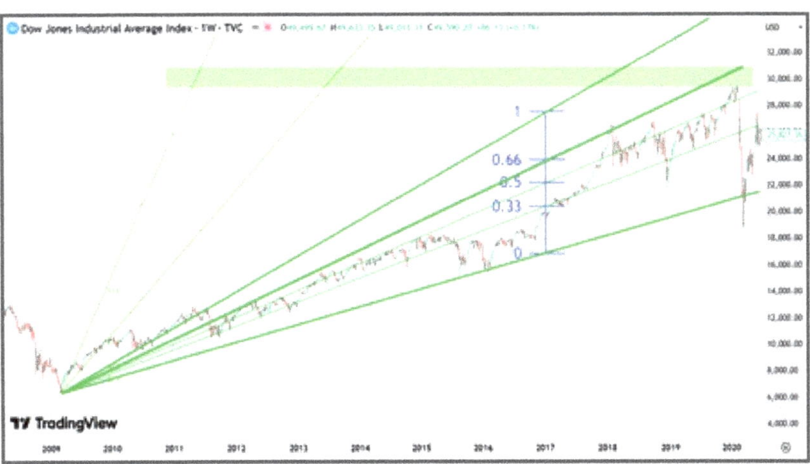

Figure 18. Subdivision of the 4/1-8/1 sector to define the 2020 market top.

These time points can then be reinforced with fans from other market lows as we did in Figure 16. Figure 19 shows the addition of three extra fans to reinforce the 66% line in Figure 18. All three of these fans needed sector sub-division. The relevant lines are in bold. The green line is 66% of the 4/1 – 8/1 sector from the 2009 low (Figure 18). The blue line is 66% of the 4/1 – 8/1 sector from the 2011 low. The red line is 33% of the 2/1 – 4/1 sector from the 2016 low. The black line is 33% of the 1/1 – 2/1 sector from the 2018 low. The black ellipse is again drawn through the price zone to encapsulate all four lines. Note the increasing slope of the last two lines and the accuracy of their time prediction.

Figure 19. Additional fan lines predicting the 2020 market top.

Market Bottoms

Using the Gann fan to find market bottoms is simpler than its use for finding market tops. A similar correlation between the fan lines and the Fibonacci retracement tool is used for this. The fan is not scaled, but simply drawn from a market low with the 1/1 line through the major market top. In this case the 3/1 line is retained. The intersection of the fan lines and the retracement levels is used to denote potential ***time/price*** market bottoms. As was carried out above, a number of fans can be drawn from the various market lows and the intersection of these fan lines can be used to reinforce selected time/price points.

Noting the date of the fan line/retracement level convergence can also increase the reliability of the forecast bottom. Gann attributed great importance to the dates of the two solstices (December 21st-22nd and June 20th-21st) and the two equinoxes (March 21st and September 23st). He further divided the year into eighths using the dates May 7th, August 7th, November 7th and February 5th. All these dates are essentially harmonic nodes (chapter 3) which he deemed to be significant times of the year.

Figures 20, 21 and 22 show the Gann fans added to the market retracements seen in Figures 4, 5 and 6.

Figure 20 shows a weekly chart of the DJI with the workup for the market bottom in 2002. The bottom was the mid-cycle retracement in the last major cycle 1987-2007. The green fan is drawn from the low in 1987 to the mid-cycle top in 2000. The blue fan is drawn, due to the lack of any significant retracement, from the prominent inflection point in 1994 from which the market rocketed up to

Figure 20. Gann fans and retracement levels indicate the market low in 2002-03.

the high in 2000. You can see that the market, the fan lines and the 38% retracement level all converge to give a good estimate of the ***time*** and ***price*** of the market bottom. Note also, the dates. The lowest low was in early October about three weeks after the September equinox. The last low (marked) was in early March just one and a half weeks before the March equinox. Note also the triple bottom/inverted head-and-shoulders pattern at this bottom. These market patterns are strong indicators of a trend change.

Figure 21 shows a similar workup for the major low of the last cycle in 2009. The fans are now drawn to the top of the market in 2007 and, since this market bottom is below all other retracements, the same inflection point is used for the second fan. The result is not as clean as in the previous figure, but you can see the convergence of the market and a fan line at the 62% retracement level. A second fan line is close by. The 62% retracement is a very powerful level as it is often the extreme point in a market move. Note again the date and the inverted head-and-shoulders pattern

Figure 21. Gann fans, retracement levels and the low of 2009.

Figure 22 shows the mid-cycle low/COVID panic in 2020. This time it is the 50% retracement level with fan lines close by. Again, note the date.

Figure 22. Gann fans, retracement levels and the COVID low in 2020.

Figure 23 shows yet another impressive example of this methodology. This is a daily chart of the DJI for the two years after the COVID low. The fans are drawn from the bottom in March 2020 to the top in January 2022, and from the low of the only significant retracement (see chapter 4) in October 2020. Note how exquisitely the fan lines cross at exactly the 38% level on the Friday before the solstice. Note also that at this level, the market had retraced back to the 2020 high in a classic breakout pattern. This daily low in the Australian market was the lowest point of the retracement. But in the American market, despite making the new higher high in August 2022, there was another low in September/October 2022. This sometimes happens when using Gann price/time techniques. The significant Gann high/low may not always be the extreme high/low, but it will be close to it, so decisions made at these time points will not be far from the mark. The significance of using the Gann fan tool in this way can also be seen by the manner in which the market movement respects these lines.

In the last two chapters we have enhanced two drawing tools that are found in every charting package with numbers and ratios that are repeatedly found in Gann's work. These tools and ratios are particularly suited to analysis of the DJI. If using these enhanced

Figure 23. Post COVID Gann fans and retracement levels intersecting at the June solstice 2022.

tools is all you ever do, you will be well placed to better time the major market tops and bottoms. Nevertheless, I regard this chapter and the earlier chapters as essentially technical in nature. Like all technical systems, these approaches do not work all the time. You have to know ***when*** to use them. In the following chapters we will explore more fully the time cycles that are relevant to the DJI and approach the timing of market tops from a different perspective. Only by understanding the cyclic nature of this market can we use the technical knowledge from these earlier chapters to best effect. Knowing ***when*** a market top is due, and understanding ***where*** you are in that cycle is the real power of Gann's approach to investing.

Part 2

Discovering the Esoteric

Chapter 6
Planetary Cycles

The use of time cycles is what sets WD Gann's work apart from other market traders. The concept that time is circular, not linear. Gann thought of everything as having a cycle: you, me, companies, markets, everything. And each of these cycles he linked to the heavens, to specific planetary movements and cycles.

I remind you of his thoughts on this matter from chapter seven of TTTTA, page 76 where he says "this makes it plain that everything works according to past cycles, and that history repeats itself in the lives of men, nations and the stock market".

This concept allows us to look back to the past at specific, repeating blocks time which contain similar characteristics. In identifying the timing of these characteristics it is then possible to forecast future events. In the case of the share market, and in particular the DJI, the characteristics we are looking for in this book are the timings of the major tops and bottoms of the market cycle.

In this chapter we will work through some of the cycles that are relevant to the major highs and lows of DJI.

The Land Cycle (The Moon's North Node Cycle)

Mainstream economics suggests that the economic cycles are driven by things like interest rates, inflation, company profits, employment, wages, house prices, living costs. Changes in these factors are what we "see" and "feel" over the cycle, but they do not cause the cycle. They are the ***result*** of the cycle.

The main driver of the boom-bust economic cycle is ***the price of land***. The land cycle has been documented for 200 years in the USA and longer in Europe. There is a sub-group of authors and commentators world-wide who have discovered and written about this cycle for the over 100 years. Some of these authors have also explained how a change in the way that economics is taught has denied an understanding of this cycle to the general public and also (sadly) to the people who run the world economies.

To start our study of the land cycle, some of the key people and publications are listed below in chronological order. This list is by no means extensive. There is a large pool of literature and authors, both past and present that awaits the curious researcher. But for now, this short list will suffice as a summary of the principles and history of the land cycle.

Henry George (1839-97) was an American economist and journalist. He pondered the paradox of increasing inequality and poverty in the midst of economic and technological progress. He recognized that land values were the cause of this inequity. As the population grows, land values grow and we all must pay more to live and work on it. He recognized that land speculation drove the land price out of the reach of the ordinary citizen. In his most famous work "Progress and Poverty" (1879) he proposed a solution to the boom/bust business cycle with a single land tax to replace many of our other taxes. He claimed this would "level the playing field" by holding land values more constant and create more social equality.

This theme was also picked up by others including Winston Churchill and David Lloyd George who proposed a similar tax. But the "People's Budget" was ultimately not accepted. Land ownership and the concept of increasing land prices was well engrained into "the establishment" and eventually they won the debate. So to this day the world's economies continue to go through the same boom/bust cycles with devastating consequences for most ordinary people.

In Australia, the gap between the (property) "haves" and the "have-nots" is perhaps most vividly seen in a 2003 quote by the Prime Minister John Howard in which he said "I don't get people stopping me in the street and saying, 'John you're outrageous, under your government the value of my house has increased!'"

However despite world government inaction, there is a lesson to be learned here. The lesson is that knowing the ***solution*** to the problem lets us better define the ***cause*** of the problem. The problem is the continuing boom/bust economic cycles. The cause is land speculation which drives the land price to unsustainable levels, precipitating an economic collapse.

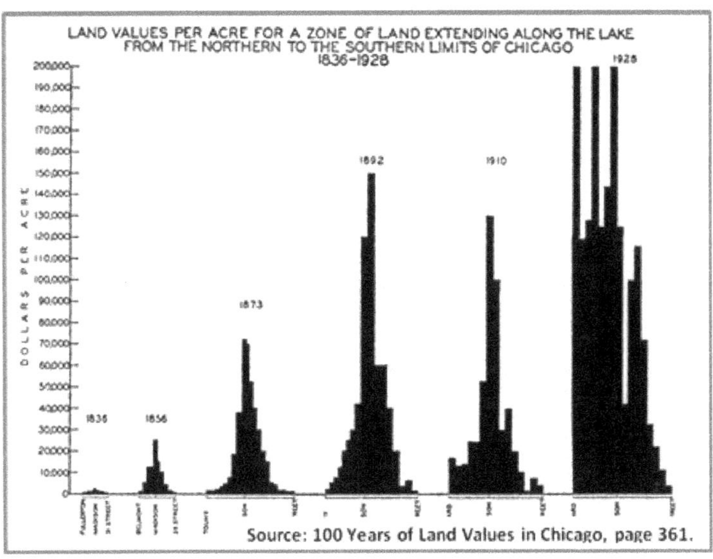

Figure 24. Land price peaks in Chicago 1836-1928.

One of the first objective studies to document the land cycle was published in 1933. Homer Hoyt was an American economist known for his work on land use planning and zoning. In 1933 he published a book titled "100 Years of Land Values in Chicago". This book records the changes in Chicago land prices from 1830 to 1933. Figure 24 is from page 361 of his book which shows the land price between 1836 and 1928. Note the rhythmic, pulse-like peaks which resulted from bursts of land speculation driving land prices to extraordinary levels. This is the land cycle. The average length of Chicago's cycle was 18.4 years. You should understand that the collapse of the land price after each peak is associated with a major economic collapse.

In 1983 Fred Harrison published "The Power in the Land". Fred is a British journalist/writer and in this book he also proposed an 18 year property cycle, with 14 years of rising values follow by 4 years of lower land prices before a market recovery. The 14 year portion of the cycle was based on the long term interest rates and the ability of the individual to pay off their mortgage. Using this cycle, Fred successfully predicted the 2008 GFC back in the 1990's, more than a decade before it happened.

Fred has written several other books and in 1994 he co-authored a book with Mason Gaffney who was Professor of Economics at the University of California at the time. The book is titled "The Corruption of Economics" and it describes how the powerful elite countered Henry George's ideas by hiring academics to change economic teaching. This change involved removing the "land" from the economic dogma which deprived economists the ability to diagnose problems and forecast trends, but allowed those with property to continue to benefit from land price growth. So without an understanding of the role of the land, this corrupted economic teaching condemned the 20th century to continuing boom/bust cycles.

The folly of ignoring (land) cycles in the management of our economy was highlighted in 1967 by Edward Dewey. He was appointed chief economic analyst in 1931 by President Hoover to elucidate the cause of the great depression which occurred after the 1928 land cycle peak. In 1941 he was instrumental in forming the "Foundation for the Study of Cycles". His 1967 book "The case for Cycles" made this observation: "insofar as cycles are meaningful, all science that has been ***developed in the absence of cycle knowledge is inadequate and partial***. Thus, if cyclic forces are real, any theory of ***economics***, or sociology, or history, or medicine, or climatology that ignores non-chance rhythms is manifestly incomplete, as medicine was before the discovery of germs".

This corrupted economic teaching is still in place in the 21st century. The concept of a land cycle is completely foreign to the banking and economic professionals. Politicians are even worse. They all just blunder along with no concept of what has happened before and what will happen again. All because the "land" has been removed from economic theory.

More recent, 21st century authors include:

Phillip J Anderson who, in 2008, published "The Secret Life of Real Estate and Banking: How it Moves and Why". Phil is a Melbourne-born Australian who now travels the world promoting his findings. His book is very large and comprehensive, and details an 18.6 year cycle with 14 years of growth followed by 4.6 years recession/depression. Phil also produces a subscription service for those who wish to understand the cycle. I subscribed to Phil's newsletter for many years. His writings are one of the main reasons I started my journey into Gann. One significant addition in his book is that he divides the 14 growth years into two periods of ***seven*** years with what he describes as a "mid-cycle slow down/recession" in the middle. The cycle he describes is, again, a land-based cycle rather than a share market cycle, but he points out that the two cycles are linked as the collapse of inflated land values and the subsequent effect on the banking sector, acts as the major catalyst to bring down the whole share market. The share market tends to crash after the top of the land cycle, but then recovers more quickly as the banking sector and the real estate market take a few years to wash out the bad debts.

Catherine Cashmore is a UK born, Melbourne based writer. She has been writing about the Australian property market for many years. Whilst mainly property focused, she has not lost sight of the underlying land cycle that drives the market. Her knowledge of history, network of contacts with their novel statistics and online interviews helps grow market/cycle knowledge for all who are interested.

At the time of writing Akhil Patel has just published a book titled "The Secret Wealth Advantage" (2023). Akhil is Phillip Anderson's business partner. This book documents the 18 year (land) cycle and suggests strategies to take advantage of the various parts of the cycle. Knowing and understanding the cycle allows great benefit to be gained from the key time points.

In the past, many counties had their own separate land cycles. Whilst the world's share markets tend to collapse in unison with the US market, the land cycles have often been out of synch. In Australia the land cycle has peaked after the last three share market tops. So it has been the ***US land cycle*** that has correlated best with the market movements. But the offsets in different county's land cycles are changing. With increased communication, the whole world is now progressively moving towards one synchronized cycle. The growth of the internet was initially responsible for this, but the development of the smart phone (since the last market top in 2007) has accelerated our ability to communicate exponentially. We walk around with high powered computers in our pockets and can obtain information from anywhere in the world at any time. This instant communication helps drive the cycle.

It is uncertain if Gann knew about the land cycle, but in 1909 he published his Financial Timetable which has a cycle length of 18.6 years. This cycle matches exactly the land cycle described by the above authors. And, in a link to the heavens, Gann's cycle is based on the movement of the Moon's north node.

The Moon's north node was included in the price scaling exercise cited in the last chapter. The node is not a planet, but a point in space at the intersection of the Earth's and the Moon's planes of orbit. These orbital planes are slightly angled to each other so that, as the Moon revolves around the Earth each month, there is a point at which the Moon moves up through the Earth's plane of orbit and a second point at which it moves down through the Earth's plane. These are the two nodes of the Moon. The ascending node or north node is what is referred to as "the Moon's node". This point in the heavens moves steadily backwards through the Zodiac with a cycle time of 18.6 years.

In Figure 25, I have reproduced Gann's 1909 Financial Time Table which has been cropped to make it more legible.

FINANCIAL TIME TABLE						compiled by W.D.Gann (1909)			
1840	1858	1877	1895	1914	1932	1951	1969	1988	
1841A	1859A	1878A	1896A	1915A	1933A	1952A	1970A	1989A	A - Extreme low
1842	1860	1879	1897	1916	1934	1953	1971	1990	despair, begi
1843	1861	1880	1898	1917	1935	1954	1972	1991	of 18.6 years, improving bu
1844	1862	1881	1899	1918	1936	1955	1973	1992	
1845B	1863B	1882B	1900B	1919B	1937B	1956B	1974B	1993B	B - High stock pri
1846	1864	1883	1901	1920	1938	1957	1975	1994	
1847C	1865C	1884C	1902C	1921C	1939C	1958C	1976C	1995C	C - Panic
1848D	1866D	1885D	1903D	1922D	1940D	1959D	1977D	1996D	D - Low stock pri
1849	1867	1886	1904	1923	1941	1960	1978	1997	
1850E	1868	1887E	1905	1924E	1942	1961E	1979	1998E	E - High stock pri
1851F	1869E	1888F	1906E	1925F	1943E	1962F	1980E	1999F	F - Panic
1852	1870F	1889	1907F	1926	1944F	1963	1981F	2000	
1853G	1871G	1890G	1908G	1927G	1945G	1964G	1982G	2001G	G - Low stock pri
1854H	1872	1891H	1909	1928H	1946	1965H	1983	2002H	H - Very high sto
1855	1873H	1892	1910H	1929	1947H	1966	1984H	2003	most money i
1856J	1874J	1893J	1911J	1930J	1948J	1967J	1985J	2004J	J - Major panic C
1857	1875	1894	1912	1931	1949	1968	1986	2005	prices,busine
1858	1876	1895	1913	1932	1950	1969	1987	2006	kitchens, disp
1859K	1877	1896K	1914	1933K	1951	1970K	1988	2007K	K - Same as A plu
1860	1878K	1897	1915K	1934	1952K	1971	1989K	2008	prominent de
							Source: Internet & PSS		

Figure 25. Gann's financial time table.

If you know the history of the DJI, you will note how well the years in the "K" rows align with the bottom of the major market downturns. It is truly amazing that Gann was able to predict the 2008 GFC one hundred years before it happened. Such is the market forecasting power of the correct time cycle.

Although there is a good correlation between Gann's nodal cycle and the land cycle described above, these "big picture" approaches do not make it easy to track the cycle. Fortunately, in our internet-based world, the relevant data are available to everyone if you know where to look.

Finding the underlying land cycle is really the first crucial step in understanding where we are in the economic cycle. Land price/ real estate data are available from a number of sources including TradingEconomics.com or TradingView.com. You need to be careful as many of the real estate based charts are distorted by the overall share market movements. But there are some indices which show "clean" data. One such index is the Case-Shiller 20-city Home Price Index (Figure 26) which measures the residential house prices in ***20 US cities***. This index only shows data from January 2000, but it does provide accurate information about the last and the present US land cycles.

Figure 26. The Case-Schiller 20-city composite home price index.

The bottom of the previous US land cycle was in 1992. If we apply Anderson's criteria, to get to the mid-point of the cycle we add seven years which takes us to 1999. The share market subsequently peaked in January of 2000 before the mid-cycle slow down which bottomed out in 2002. If we then add another seven years (fourteen years in total) we come to 2006. Figure 26 clearly shows the peak of the land cycle in 2006 (red arrow). The share market peaked a year later in 2007 as the land prices were declining which precipitated the start of the GFC and the eventual share market bottom in 2009.

However, despite the start of a recovery in the DJI from 2009, you can see that the land market took a few more years to bottom out which it did in 2012 (green arrow), marking the start of the present cycle. If we add seven years to 2012 we get 2019, and again the share market peaked in early 2020 before the mid-cycle slow down which was exacerbated by the COVID pandemic. However, this market correction was not another market top/GFC because there was no collapse of the land prices. Further to this you can see the inflection point in the market around the start of 2021 as the land prices increase their upward trajectory through the second part of the cycle. It is only by adding another seven years (2012 + 14 years) to 2026 that we see a potential land cycle top, with a share market top expected soon thereafter.

Another significant index is the ***US Building Permits***. This data is also readily available and it has the added advantage of extending back to the 1960's (Figure 27). The peaks and troughs of this graph are slightly offset (to the left) from the data of Figure 26 because building permits tend to peak before land prices. Nevertheless, you can still clearly see the last 14 year cycle (1991-2005) and the start of the present cycle (~2011-).

The critical point about these data is that they are ***leading indicators***. Most share market indicators are based on the past price history of the share/commodity. So using them to predict the future is a bit like driving a car whilst looking in the rear vision mirror. A true leading indicator independently predicts the market movement. Figure 27 shows the building permit peak in 1984-86 (red circle) ***before*** the 1987 market collapse and the 2005 peak ***before*** the 2007 downturn. Combining the data in Figures 26 and 27 allows us to see the exquisite cascade of the last cycle with the building permits peak in 2005 followed by the land price peak in 2006, both prior to the share market peak in 2007. You can also see the start of the present cycle with the building permits bottoming for a second time in 2011, a year before the home price index in 2012.

Figure 27. The US building permits.

Returning to Gann's forecast (Figure 25), it is now worth gaining an improved perspective on his financial cycle by incorporating our knowledge of the land cycle with the Moon's nodal cycle. It is unclear if Gann was working with knowledge of the land cycle when he published his Financial Timetable as Homer Hoyt had not yet published his book. This potentially gives us an advantage that Gann did not have. In addition, the DJI at that time was only thirteen years old. Today it is nearly 130 years old with over six nodal cycles completed which provides plenty of time and price data to analyse.

As mentioned, the Moon's node precesses (moves backwards) at a regular pace through the signs of the zodiac taking 18.6 years to make one revolution. Figure 28 shows its position at 7° Aquarius and its direction of movement (R = retrograde) at the bottom of the last cycle on March the 6th 2009. This market bottom was the disastrous end of the last cycle. The K rows of Gann's forecast table are all major cycle bottoms and are all closely associated with the node in Aquarius. This node/Aquarius association with destruction has been known for millennia. Ancient Hindu and Buddhist texts talk of Rahu (the Moon's north node) swallowing the Sun and the Moon. This refers to the solar and lunar eclipses which occur when the Moon's node is between the Earth and the Sun. Most ancient cultures viewed these events with great fear and trepidation. And as a result, Hindu astrology considered the node to be a malefic planet which, pertinent to our discussion here, was considered to rule the sign of Aquarius. Gann undoubtedly learned of this ancient association is his travels. However, it must be remembered that the destructive end of one market cycle is also the beginning of the next cycle. This was a key time point for Gann who placed great importance in knowing the starting point of a cycle as a reference to predict the future movements.

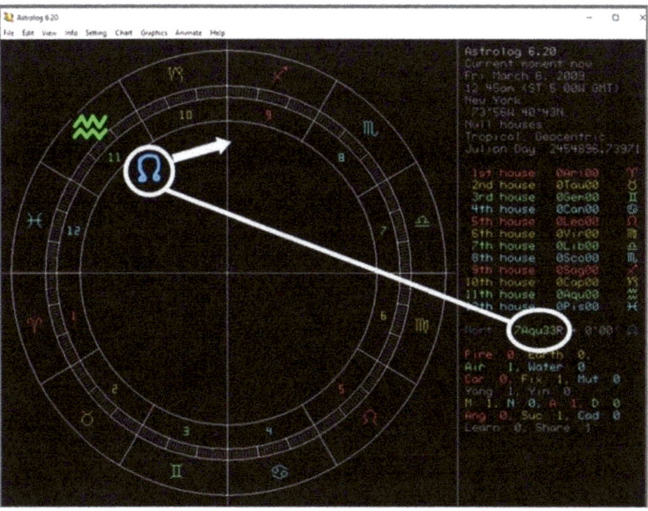

Figure 28. Astrolog chart showing the Moon's node at 7° Aquarius on March 6th 2009.

To visualize the performance of the DJI for the last 130 years, in Figure 29 I have taken Gann's financial timetable and re-annotated it. Along the top of the table you can see the yearly structure of the timetable by displaying the alternating 18 and 19 year differences at the start of each column. These time frames average out to 18.5 years which is very close to the 18.6 year nodal cycle. The extra 0.1 of a year produces a "catch up" year every 10 cycles with two cycles in a row showing a 19 year difference. I have also extended the time frame for two more cycles to the year 2045 to include the current cycle.

The start of the Dow Jones Index in 1896 is indicated and I have attempted to colour code the end of cycle years, the obvious up years and the obvious down years. Significant highs and lows are also highlighted.

On top of all this I have also included the position of the node at critical time points. We have already discussed the bottom of the market with the node in Aquarius, but prior to this point, the top of the market is associated with the node in Pisces. Remember the node is precessing backwards through the zodiac. Pisces is a Water sign while Aquarius is an Air sign. Now if you are familiar with astrology and the zodiac you will know that there are two other pairs of Water/Air signs: Scorpio/Libra and Cancer/Gemini. I have included all three pairs of Water/Air signs using blue/green bars in the years following the Second World War.

You can now see the close association of the last three major cycle tops and bottoms with the node in Pisces and then Aquarius, including the potential for the next top in 2025-26 and the next bottom in 2027-28. We will discuss the timing of these major tops and bottoms further in the next chapter.

Leaving the major tops and bottoms for the moment, it should be noted that the other Water/Air pairs are also very interesting. The "mid-cycle slowdown", which is in the middle of upswing of start of DJI 1896 at cycle low

	18	19	18	19	18	19	18	19	19	18		
1840	1858	1877	1895	**1914**	**1932**	1951	1969	**1988**	**2007**	2025		
1841	1859	1878	**1896**	**1915**	**1933**	**1952**	**1970**	**1989**	**2008**	2026	A	Extreme low in Aquarius
1842	1860	1879	1897	**1916**	1934	**1953**	1971	**1990**	**2009**	2027		
1843	1861	1880	1898	**1917**	1935	1954	1972	1991	2010	2028		
1844	1862	1881	**1899**	1918	1936	1955	**1973**	1992	2011	2029	B	Rising/high prices through Scorpio
1845	1863	1882	1900	**1919**	**1937**	1956	**1974**	1993	2012	2030		
1846	1864	1883	**1901**	1920	1938	1957	1975	1994	2013	2031		
1847	1865	1884	1902	**1921**	1939	1958	1976	1995	**2014**	2032	C	Retracement low through Libra
1848	1866	1885	**1903**	1922	1940	1959	1977	1996	**2015**	2033		
1849	1867	1886	1904	1923	1941	1960	1978	1997	2016	2034		
1850	1868	1887	1905	1924	**1942**	**1961**	1979	1998	2017	2035	D	Rising/high prices through Cancer
1851	1869	1888	**1906**	1925	1943	**1962**	1980	1999	2018	2036		
1852	1870	1889	**1907**	1926	1944	1963	**1981**	**2000**	2019	2037		
1853	1871	1890	1908	1927	1945	1964	**1982**	2001	**2020**	2038	E	Mid-cycle low through Gemini
1854	1872	1891	**1909**	1928	**1946**	**1965**	1983	**2002**	2021	2039		
1855	1873	1892	1910	**1929**	1947	**1966**	1984	2003	**2022**	2040		
1856	1874	1893	1911	1930	1948	1967	1985	2004	2023	2041	F	Rising/high prices through Pisces
1857	1875	1894	1912	1931	**1949**	**1968**	1986	2005	2024	2042		
1858	1876	1895	1913	**1932**	1950	1969	**1987**	2006	2025	2043		
1859	1877	1896	**1914**	**1933**	1951	**1970**	**1988**	**2007**	2026	2044	G	Major crash in Aquarius
1860	1878	1897	**1915**	1934	**1952**	1971	**1989**	**2008**	2027	2045		

node in Pis, Sco, Can — up years — **1915** major lows

node in Aqu, Lib, Gem — down years — **1919** major highs

end of cycle years

Source: PSS

Figure 29. Re-annotation of Gann's financial time table.

the ***land cycle***, is actually two thirds of the way through the share market cycle and corresponds to the node being in Cancer for a market top followed by Gemini for the market bottom. This offset of one cycle within the other is due to the delay in the formation of a bottom in the land cycle as discussed above.

The third Water/Air sign pair is never discussed. Yet you can see that the market tends to have a minor high followed by a retracement as the node moves through Scorpio and Libra. This is most noticeable in the current cycle with a high in 2014-15 and lows in 2015-16.

So like the land cycle, the current share market cycle from 2009 is also a text book example of the cycle timings. Figure 30 shows the DJI for the last twenty years overlaid with the nodal Water/Air sign timings. You can see the last mid-cycle slowdown 2000-2003, the major high of 2007 followed by the GFC into 2009, the minor high and retracement of 2015-16, and the recent mid-cycle slowdown/ COVID crash of 2020.

Figure 30. Twenty years of the DJI overlaid with the nodal timings.

The Jupiter/Saturn Cycle

The Jupiter/Saturn synodic cycle is both a twenty year cycle and a sixty year cycle. And for Gann these 20/60 year time frames were major cycle periods. Approximately every twenty years Jupiter and Saturn are conjunct in the night sky. The planes of orbit for these two planets are not perfectly aligned so they do not eclipse each other. Rather, they are conjunct when they occupy the same longitude in the zodiac. At the solstice on 21st and 22nd of December 2020 these two large planets could be seen one directly above the other in the night sky. This constituted a major shift or mutation in the cycle as for the last two hundred years these planets have met in the Earth signs of Taurus, Virgo and Capricorn. But from 2020 for the next two hundred years they will be conjunct in the Air signs (Aquarius, Gemini and Libra) of the zodiac. Due to the differences in their orbital periods, the conjunctions of these planets will step between the three Air signs in a double trine (240°) movement from Aquarius, to Libra and then Gemini. It will be sixty years (3 twenty year cycles) before they again meet in Aquarius.

In his book Astro-Cycles and Speculative Markets, Luther J Jensen discusses the Jupiter/Saturn conjunction cycle. He suggests a relationship between economic prosperity/depression and the geometry in the zodiac of the three, slowly moving planets Jupiter, Saturn and Uranus. So it is worthwhile to examine (in addition to the nodal cycle) this 20 year cycle in relation to the movement of the share market.

Examination of the Jupiter/Saturn conjunction cycle reveals that despite it being labelled as a "20 year" cycle, the cycles actually show some variation. Unlike the Moon's node, the orbits of Jupiter and Saturn are elliptical so the cycle times vary from one cycle to the next. The average cycle is 20 years, but the real cycle times vary from a low of 19.4 years to a high of 20.6 years. Figure 31 shows the geocentric conjunction cycles since the beginning of the DJI together with the market tops from Figure 29. These market tops occur on average, seven years after the prior conjunction, with the three post-second world war tops occurring precisely seven years after a conjunction. It is tantalising to suggest the next market high might be in 2027, seven years after the 2020 conjunction. These red market tops are the last major highs in each column before the ("K" row) green market lows. They therefore should be regarded as the major market tops which precede the end of cycle collapse. You can see that they run on the diagonal, getting progressively later each cycle with only the last two highs aligning exactly with the Moon's node is in Pisces. The position of the 1946 top can be forgiven due to the effect of the second world-war. So whilst Gann's financial forecast appears to be accurate in predicting the major cycle lows, it may be less accurate with the cycle highs. Figure 31 is suggestive of another pattern for the cycle highs which is associated with the Jupiter/Saturn cycle. This will be discussed further in the next chapter.

Conjunction	Cycle (years)	Market tops						
19/4/1881								
29/11/1901	20.6	1909	1909	1928	1946	1965	1983	**2002**
12/09/1921	19.8	1929	1910	1929	1947	**1966**	1984	2003
18/02/1941	19.4	1946	1911	1930	1948	1967	1985	2004
18/02/1961	20.0	1968	1912	1931	**1949**	1968	1986	2005
28/12/1980	19.9	1987	1913	**1932**	1950	1969	1987	2006
28/05/2000	19.4	2007	**1914**	**1933**	1951	**1970**	**1988**	2007
21/12/2020	20.6							
1/11/2040	19.9							

Source: PSS

Figure 31. Jupiter/Saturn conjunctions and the DJI market tops.

The Uranus Cycle (The War Cycle)

Jensen also talks at length about the Uranus cycle which he describes as "the cycles of approximately 84 years that have been so closely identified with American life". He documents the first Spanish settlement of mainland America in 1523 with Uranus at 8-9° Gemini. Eighty four years later in 1607 sees the first English settlement at Jamestown, Virginia. In 1691 there is political and religious dissension resulting in the burning of Jamestown. In 1775 the seeds of American independence were sown with the declaration of independence signed on July 4th 1776 with Uranus again at 9° Gemini. Another 84 years sees the Uranus oscillating backwards and forwards across 7-9° Gemini from 1859 to 1861 when the first armed conflict of the civil war took place.

Jensen's book was originally written in 1935 and he described the phenomenon of Uranus at 7-9° Gemini as the "unexplained and unique North American continental point". He hypothesized that the years 1943-45 (84 years after the civil war) would be "the most momentous period so far encountered in American history". These, of course, are the years of the second world war into which America was dragged after the attack on Pearl Harbour.

At the time of writing we are four years away from Uranus again being at 7-9° Gemini in 2027-28. It is likely that this too will herald another difficult time for America, the American economy and therefore for the world economy. A physical war could disrupt the share market cycle as it did during the second world war. But "war" does not necessarily mean armed conflict. Cyber conflict is increasingly becoming a significant way to disrupt the economy of a country and cause chaos. Astrologists will tell you that Uranus in Gemini will bring upheaval to communication and technology. Such a scenario may simply exacerbate the market downturn and delay any recovery. Either way, the years leading up to 2027 need to be watched carefully for signs which could affect the timing of the market top.

The Kondratiev Cycle

This cycle is not a planetary cycle, it is a commodity cycle. Nikolai Kondratiev was a Russian economist who was born in 1892 and is known for his theory of long-term economic cycles. He advocated a market-led industrialisation strategy for Russia which was in contradiction to Joseph Stalin who favoured complete government control of the economy. He was also at odds with the Marxist idea that capitalism would ultimately collapse. For his views on the Russian economy Nikolai was imprisoned and ultimately executed at the age of 46.

Kondratiev studied the prices of many things including raw materials, output products, interest rates and wages resulting in the theory of a major economic/commodity cycle of 50-60 years duration. This cycle had two phases with a 25-30 year up phase followed by a 25-30 year decline. He documented that wars and revolutions tended to occur during the up phase of the cycle. This is because the increased need for commodities near the top of the cycle caused prices to rise and this ***exacerbated geo-political tensions.***

Kondratiev's data goes back to the 1700's and now demonstrates four completed cycles with the low of the last cycle around the turn of the last century in the year 2000. So the top of the present up wave should occur in the late 2020's in concert with the land, share market and Uranus cycles. This timing is yet another reason to be vigilant over the next few years.

In this chapter we have taken a first step into Gann's esoteric world by introduced two of his planetary cycles. Using the Moon's node and the Jupiter/Saturn cycles we have suggested a big picture method for forecasting the major market cycle tops and bottoms. These big picture approaches do not always align in the way we would like because of differences in the cycle timings. Nevertheless, both these cycles have brought us to a similar time point of 2026-2027 for the potential top of the current cycle. Knowing roughly when the market top is expected allows you to use the technical methodologies discussed in the earlier chapters to zero in on more accurate time and price points. In the next chapter we will consider additional ways to augment this big picture cycle knowledge as we take a further step into Gann's world.

Chapter 7
Natal Astrology

Gann was a master astrologer and he used astrology in much of his trading. Astrology can get very involved with the inclusion of planetary nature, the personality of each sign of the zodiac, planetary rulerships of each house and so on. In this chapter we are going to leave this detail aside and simply define astrology as the position of the planets within the twelve houses of the zodiac. However, even using this simplified definition does not let us escape the complexity of this form of analysis. Some people may struggle with this chapter.

The day we are born the planets are in a particular pattern in the zodiac. This is our natal chart. The word natal means "of or associated with the beginning" and Gann put great store in knowing the beginning point. Events in our lives can be tracked to the movement of the planets relative to their positions in our natal chart. The same can be said of countries with the association of the 84 year Uranus cycle to the USA already discussed. And the same can also be said for companies and businesses. This association of planetary movement relative to a known starting point is at the heart of Gann's time cycles and his trading approach.

In this chapter we will use natal astrology to look for repeating patterns and/or positions of planets within the zodiac rather than using a simple yearly time count. Unknowingly we have already done this in the last chapter with the nodal cycle where a single 360° retrograde cycle (18.6 Earth years) is seen to describe the major economic cycle. The bottom of the market is seen consistently to coincide with the node in Aquarius. However, if we review the last reworked version of Gann's financial timetable (Figure 29), we find that the tops of the market (the red major highs immediately before the major lows) are not horizontally arranged but appear to run on a diagonal. This suggests there may be other planetary associations with the market tops. In the last chapter, I alluded to an apparent relationship between the post war market highs and the Jupiter/Saturn conjunctions. This, together with Jensen's implication of the importance of the planets Jupiter, Saturn and Uranus, makes further investigation warranted.

Further to this, the main driver for the investigations in this chapter came from a post by Olga Morales. Olga is a Melbourne girl who runs a web site www.astrologyforganntraders.com.au. I don't know Olga and I have never met her, but I have bought some of her literature. On May the 1st 2010 she posted "Looking Back with W.D. Gann – Long Term Cycles" (at the time of writing this post is still available on www.astro-analyst.com). In this post Olga compared the position of Jupiter, Saturn and Uranus (Jensen's planets) at the tops and bottoms of the market in 1929, 1932 and 1987. She displayed the relationship of these 3 planets at the four time points using a quad-wheel comparative astrological chart. This feature is the essence of natal astrology as it allows analysis of planetary aspects ***across time***.

I found Olga's post in 2018, eight years after she wrote it. In 2018 my journey into Gann was not sufficiently advanced for me to understand the implication of her writings. But with time my understanding increased and I finally have recognized the power of using natal astrology.

Astrolog

We are going to use Astrolog to visualize the positions of the planets within the zodiac. We have seen a screen shot from Astrolog in the last chapter, but we are about to use this program in a more sophisticated manner so a review of the basic setup is warranted.

Astrolog is a free, down loadable program from the internet. There is help to use this program available on the internet, but I will list the setup of a few of the basic features needed to get started.

Since we are examining the cycles in the DJI, you should set the chart location to New York at a 5W time zone using (from the dropdown menu) - *Info/Set Chart Info*.

The house system should be set at "null" – *Setting/House System/Null.*

The Tropical Zodiac should be used not the Sidereal Zodiac – *Setting/Sidereal Zodiac* should not be ticked.

A Heliocentric or Geocentric view of the planets can be selected by ticking or un-ticking "Heliocentric" – *Setting/Heliocentric.*

The relevant planets can be selected in the dropdown menu by un-ticking– *Setting/Restrictions*.

The required planetary aspects can be displayed by un-ticking in the dropdown menu – *Setting/Aspect Settings*.

Time period increments are selected using "$" = 1 day, "%" = 1 month, "^" = 1 year, "&" = 10 years.

Forward time increment – *"shift/+"*, backward increment "-".

A natal astrology investigation can be displayed by using a comparison chart. This feature allows up to four different time points to be displayed at the same time with the selected planets and their planetary aspects. Setup the various time points by entering the relevant chart information into each of the charts – *Info/Charts #3 and #4* and then, to display all the charts together, tick "Comparison Chart" – *Info/Comparison Chart*.

The Major Market Tops

The second half of the economic cycle can be a difficult time. Whilst everything is booming, it is normally a period of high inflation, high interest rates and high house prices, all of which creates a cost of living crisis. Towards the US share market peak the US land cycle will have topped out, but nobody will have noticed. As the land price falls, it sets in play a series of events which result in the collapse of both the property and share markets. This can be financially devastating. To avoid being caught up in this downturn you need to recognize where you are in the cycle and take action before the economic meltdown. To that end, in this chapter I am going to use natal astrology to pin point the DJI market tops by following on from Olga's work.

In 2010 Olga demonstrated a trine (120°) relationship between the position of the planets Saturn, Jupiter and Uranus at both the top and bottom of the markets in the years 1929, 1932 and 1987. She pointed out that at these 4 different time points nearly all the planets were in the three "fire" houses of the zodiac (Aries, Sagittarius, Leo) and that the 23° position in each of these houses was a sensitive degree. The number 23 should really be included in our list of sacred numbers. Its presence astronomy and astrology is seen commonly. The Earth's axis is tilted at 23°, the solstices and equinoxes both occur on or close to the 23rd of the seasonal months, and the sun transitions to the next house of the zodiac on or about the 23rd of most months. However, in this instance, we are not going to link the number 23 to Earth seasons or months. This time we are using 23° to define a critical angular position within each house of the zodiac. Figure 32 is a reproduction of her comparison chart for these two market tops and bottoms using Astrolog.

The chart shows four concentric rings of planetary positions, with the comparative aspects in the centre. The outer ring is the top of the market in September 1929. The next ring in is the bottom of the market in July 1932. The third ring is the peak in October 1987 and the innermost ring is the bottom in October 1987 after the sudden market crash. Remarkably, the dominant aspect is the bold green trine aligned closely to the critical 23° position.

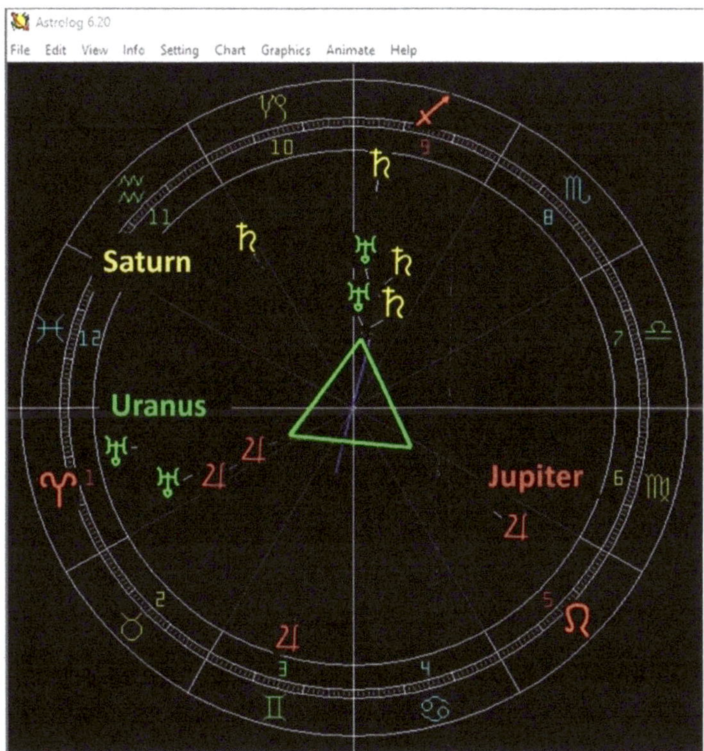

Figure 32. Jupiter, Saturn, Uranus comparison chart for September 1929 market top, July 1932 market bottom and the October 1987 top and bottom.

To take this natal comparison further, Figure 33 shows the three post second-world war market tops compared with the 1929 high. The years of these highs can be seen in Figure 29 as the last major highs before each of the market bottoms. The dates of the planetary rings in Figure 33 from the outside to the centre are September 1929, December 1968, October 1987 and July 2007. The patterns in this figure are not quite as clear as those in Figure 32, but it shows that Saturn is again consistently in a fire sign at these market tops forming a less well defined, but similar trine pattern.

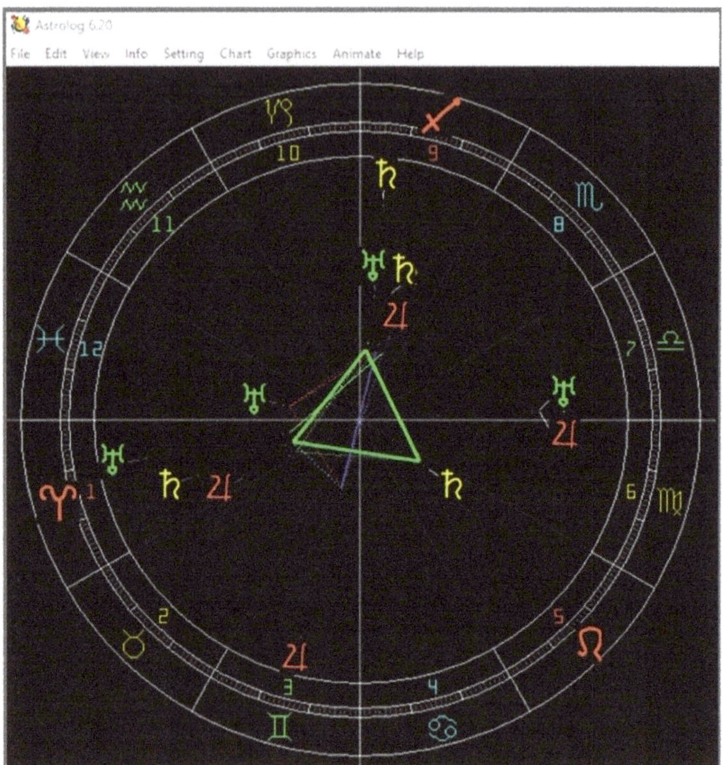

Figure 33. Jupiter, Saturn, Uranus comparison chart for the market tops in September 1929, December 1968, October 1987 and July 2007.

Gann's financial timetable shows there have been six major cycles in the DJI since its inception. Figure 33 shows planetary positions at four of better defined tops and so I wondered if there were another two tops which align with a fire sign/Saturn position. Figure 34 shows the position of Saturn in November 1909 and June 1948 which are the market highs for the cycles before and after the major 1929 peak. 1909 is one of a number of major peaks in the early 1900's and, like the post-war highs, 1909 is the last major peak before the market bottom in 1914-15 (Figure 29). It also correlates strongly with the land market peak of 1910 (Figure 24). 1948 is the least well defined high because the second-world war interfered with the speculation needed to drive the cycle. There was a market peak in 1946 in response to the end of the war, but there was also a definite, small peak in the middle of 1948. Both these peaks (1909 and 1948) coincide with Saturn in a fire sign. The dates for the planetary rings in Figure 34 are (outside to inside) December 1968, September 1929, June 1948 and November 1909. And once again the trine pattern of Saturn in the fire houses is obvious.

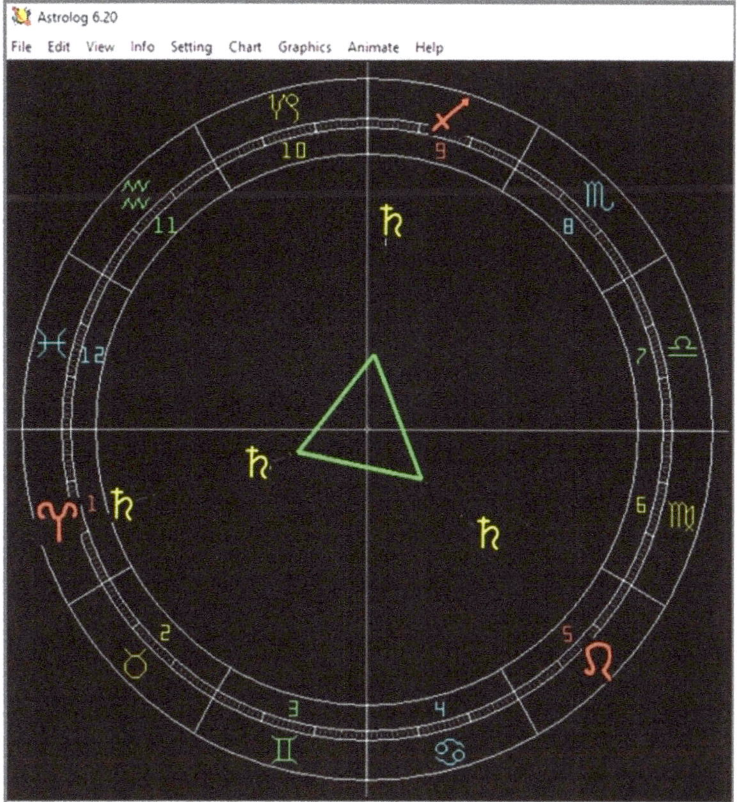

Figure 34. Saturn comparison chart for market peaks in December 1968, September 1929, June 1948 and November 1909.

So, incredibly, six major highs in the market since the inception of the DJI all occur when Saturn is in the second half (15°-30°) of a fire sign. You should note that the 23° point is in the middle of this range. In Figure 35 I have annotated the zodiac showing all six positions of Saturn at each of these highs and highlighting the trine relationship between these years. Note that the bold, trine pattern is the manifestation of our sacred number ***three***. If you follow the dates around the zodiac starting from November 1909 in Aries (moving anti-clockwise), you will find that Saturn makes a double trine move (240°) from one high to the next in a similar fashion to the double trine moves associated with the Jupiter/Saturn conjunctions. This explains the apparent relationship of the post-war highs to the conjunctions alluded to in the last chapter.

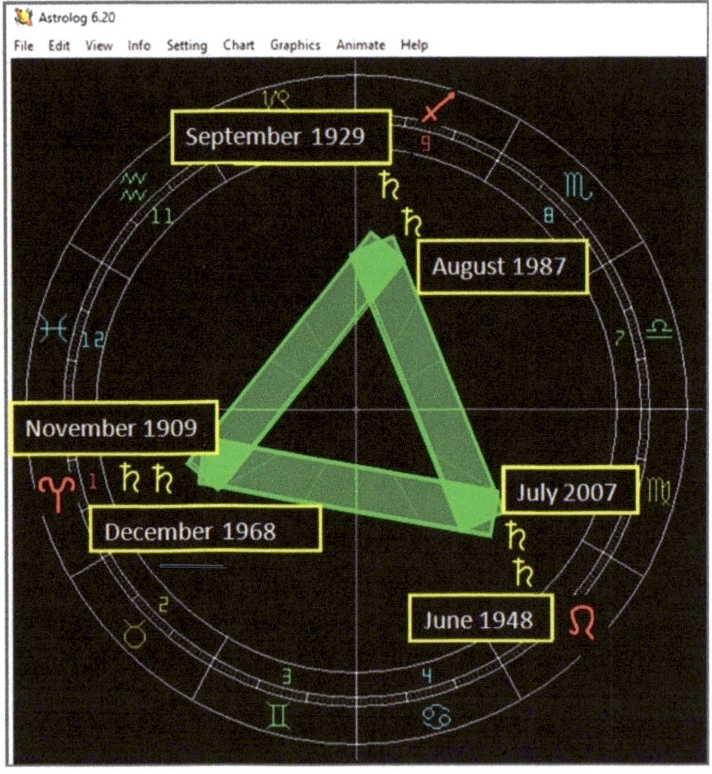

Figure 35. The zodiac annotated with the position of Saturn at the six DJI market peaks.

Visualizing this double trine Saturn cycle in context with Gann's financial forecast is seen in Figure 36. Both the heliocentric and geocentric perspectives show similar market top time windows. The heliocentric timing is shown as it is simpler than the geocentric timing which involves periods of retrograde motion. The vertical, red bars represent the time between heliocentric Saturn first passing the 15° point of the fire sign until it leaves at 30°. These lines have been extended backwards across all the years in the forecast.

Using the Saturn/fire sign cycle provides an explanation for the peak of 1929. There can be no doubt that the 1929 peak was a major market high. Whilst the 1909 and 1948 peaks only become obvious when applying the cycle, the 1929 peak is a "standout" and its position in Gann's nodal, financial time table has always bothered me. Its position is much earlier than the most recent highs. It does not line up horizontally with the 1968, 1987 or 2007 tops. Some have suggested that the pre-war market highs were originally aligned with Gann's H rows (Figure 25) and that the disruption of second world-war moved the timing of the cycle. Unfortunately, there is not enough evidence for this as the DJI had only completed 2 cycles prior to the war. Nevertheless, the precise alignment of the market tops with the Saturn/ fire sign "windows" is highly suggestive of the existence of this second cycle. The direct correlation can be seen in the history of the DJI.

However, trying to combine the Saturn cycle with the nodal cycle does produce some conflict. In Figure 36 you can see the diagonal progression of the Saturn/fire sign periods. This implies that the market peak will eventually intersect (and pass through) the bottom two rows of the table (Gann's major market lows). The end of the current DJI cycle (2026-28) may well still fit with a market peak (Saturn cycle) ahead of the market bottom (nodal cycle), but in the following cycle (2046-48) it will be interesting to see if the market peak continues to align with Saturn. Note that, in Figure 36, I have added an extra row of years to the bottom of Gann's original timetable to illustrate the Saturn/market tops into the future.

start of DJI 1896 at cycle low

1840	1858	1877	1895	1914	1932	1951	1969	1988	2007	2025
1841	1859	1878	1896	1915	1933	1952	1970	1989	2008	2026
1842	1860	1879	1897	1916	1934	1953	1971	1990	2009	2027
1843	1861	1880	1898	1917	1935	1954	1972	1991	2010	2028
1844	1862	1881	1899	1918	1936	1955	1973	1992	2011	2029
1845	1863	1882	1900	1919	1937	1956	1974	1993	2012	2030
1846	1864	1883	1901	1920	1938	1957	1975	1994	2013	2031
1847	1865	1884	1902	1921	1939	1958	1976	1995	2014	2032
1848	1866	1885	1903	1922	1940	1959	1977	1996	2015	2033
1849	1867	1886	1904	1923	1941	1960	1978	1997	2016	2034
1850	1868	1887	1905	1924	1942	1961	1979	1998	2017	2035
1851	1869	1888	1906	1925	1943	1962	1980	1999	2018	2036
1852	1870	1889	1907	1926	1944	1963	1981	2000	2019	2037
1853	1871	1890	1908	1927	1945	1964	1982	2001	2020	2038
1854	1872	1891	1909	1928	1946	1965	1983	2002	2021	2039
1855	1873	1892	1910	1929	1947	1966	1984	2003	2022	2040
1856	1874	1893	1911	1930	1948	1967	1985	2004	2023	2041
1857	1875	1894	1912	1931	1949	1968	1986	2005	2024	2042
1858	1876	1895	1913	1932	1950	1969	1987	2006	2025	2043
1859	1877	1896	1914	1933	1951	1970	1988	2007	2026	2044
1860	1878	1897	1915	1934	1952	1971	1989	2008	2027	2045
1861	1879	1898	1916	1935	1953	1972	1990	2009	2028	2046

Helio Saturn double trine moves at 15°-30° fire signs — Source: PSS

Figure 36. Gann's financial timetable annotated with Saturn/fire sign timings.

As a final step in this analysis, the financial timetable can be updated (Figure 37) by aligning horizontally the six major market tops (including 1948). Interestingly this produces an alternating 19–20 year cycle, which explains the collision course of the two cycles. Extending this cycle pattern across all the years in the timetable demonstrates Saturn's position in the fire signs and highlights the possible future market tops in 2026-27 and 2046-47. This same 19–20 year alternating cycle can be seen when following the dates around the zodiac in Figure 35.

This simple, 19-20 year alternating time count defines all the previous market tops when starting with the 1909 high.

1909 + 20 = 1929.

1929 + 19 = 1948.

1948 + 20 = 1968.

1968 + 19 = 1987.

1987 + 20 = 2007.

If this time count continues we may see:

2007 + 19 = 2026.

2026 + 20 = 2046.

start of DJI 1896 at cycle low

20	19	20	19	20	19	20	19	20	19	20
1832	1851	1871	1890	1910	1929	1949	1968	1988	2007	2027
1833	1852	1872	1891	1911	1930	1950	1969	1989	2008	2028
1834	1853	1873	1892	1912	1931	1951	1970	1990	2009	2029
1835	1854	1874	1893	1913	1932	1952	1971	1991	2010	2030
1836	1855	1875	1894	1914	1933	1953	1972	1992	2011	2031
1837	1856	1876	1895	1915	1934	1954	1973	1993	2012	2032
1838	1857	1877	1896	1916	1935	1955	1974	1994	2013	2033
1839	1858	1878	1897	1917	1936	1956	1975	1995	2014	2034
1840	1859	1879	1898	1918	1937	1957	1976	1996	2015	2035
1841	1860	1880	1899	1919	1938	1958	1977	1997	2016	2036
1842	1861	1881	1900	1920	1939	1959	1978	1998	2017	2037
1843	1862	1882	1901	1921	1940	1960	1979	1999	2018	2038
1844	1863	1883	1902	1922	1941	1961	1980	2000	2019	2039
1845	1864	1884	1903	1923	1942	1962	1981	2001	2020	2040
1846	1865	1885	1904	1924	1943	1963	1982	2002	2021	2041
1847	1866	1886	1905	1925	1944	1964	1983	2003	2022	2042
1848	1867	1887	1906	1926	1945	1965	1984	2004	2023	2043
1849	1868	1888	1907	1927	1946	1966	1985	2005	2024	2044
1850	1869	1889	1908	1928	1947	1967	1986	2006	2025	2045
1851	1870	1890	1909	1929	1948	1968	1987	2007	2026	2046
1852	1871	1891	1910	1930	1949	1969	1988	2008	2027	2047
1853	1872	1892	1911	1931	1950	1970	1989	2009	2028	2048

Helio Saturn double trine moves at 15°-30° fire signs Source: PSS

Figure 37. Gann's financial timetable with Saturn/ fire sign periods aligned horizontally.

The Major Market Bottoms

Much emphasis has been placed on timing the market tops. This is because so much financial damage can occur if you do not recognize (at the top of the market) that the economy is about to collapse. Appropriate action needs to be taken prior to this collapse if you are to survive the economic storm. Every economic cycle is bigger than the last. This is especially true of the last two cycles as the world has become a global village. The current cycle will be bigger again as more countries become synchronized into the global economy. The high will be bigger and the crash will be more violent.

The market bottoms, therefore, are the second most important part of the cycle. The recognition that the cycle has bottomed opens up the possibility of strategic investment at the best time in the cycle. Remember too that, in all probability, the share market will bottom first before the real estate cycle and the business cycle. At the bottom of the cycle the roles of the land cycle/share market cycle are reversed. The share market bottom becomes the leading indicator for the bottom of the economic cycle. So picking the share market bottom can give a critical time point on which to base a return to financial/real estate/business investment.

In this section I will again use Olga's 2010 post as the starting point for a natal astrological investigation into the major market bottoms. And for the timing of the market bottoms I am going to stay with her geocentric planetary positions. In Figure 38 the geocentric positions of Jupiter, Saturn and Uranus are shown at the market lows of 1932 and 1987 as indicated by Olga. You can see how precisely Jupiter and Uranus are aligned at 23° of the ***fire signs.*** You can also see that Jupiter and Uranus form a perfect trine across time at each of these low years. The 1932 low was prophesized by Gann on page 300 of TTTTA were he (Robert Gordon) said the war (the bull market of 1930-31) would continue until the (northern hemisphere) summer or autumn of 1932. The low of the market at that time was the 8th of July 1932.

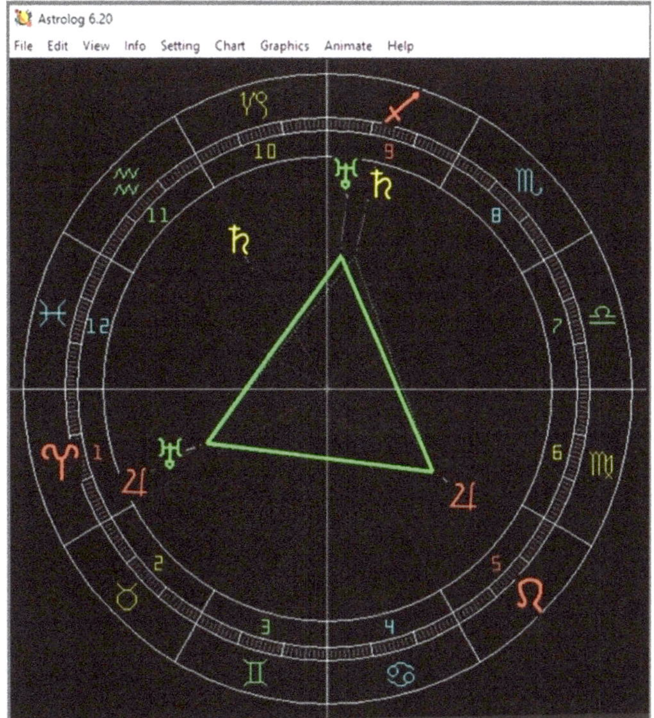

Figure 38. Jupiter, Saturn, Uranus comparison chart for the market lows of 1932 and 1987.

Over eighty years ago Jensen (Astro-cycles and Speculative Markets) suggested that critical angles (aspects) between Jupiter, Saturn and Uranus could be used to predict times of prosperity and depression. Clearly these two major lows comply with that suggestion with a perfect trine between Jupiter and Uranus on each occasion. But is it the planetary aspect or the planetary positions that define the low?

Before we move on with this investigation we need to recognize that the lows of 1932 and 1987 are separated by three major cycles (55 years in this case) and that they both occurred after market highs with Saturn in Sagittarius (Figure 35). So using our knowledge of the major market highs (above), we are going to examine the other market lows in two parts, the lows after the Saturn/Leo highs and the lows after the Saturn/Aries highs.

The market lows after the Saturn/Leo highs provide an extra opportunity to visualize the planetary pattern. Although there have been six major cycles in the DJI since its inception, the index started at a major low in 1896. If you follow the Saturn/fire sign highs backwards from the present, you will find that the 1896 low would have been after a Saturn/Leo high had the index started earlier. So we actually have seven major market lows in the DJI historic data with three lows after Saturn/Leo highs. Figure 39 shows the planetary arrangement at these time points. Incredibly, you can see the bold trine relationship between the positions of Uranus at each of these lows. Remember, each of these lows is separated by three cycles. Nevertheless, it appears that the market lows occurring after a Saturn/Leo high are all best defined by the position of Uranus, which is again at about 23°, but this time in each of the ***water signs.***

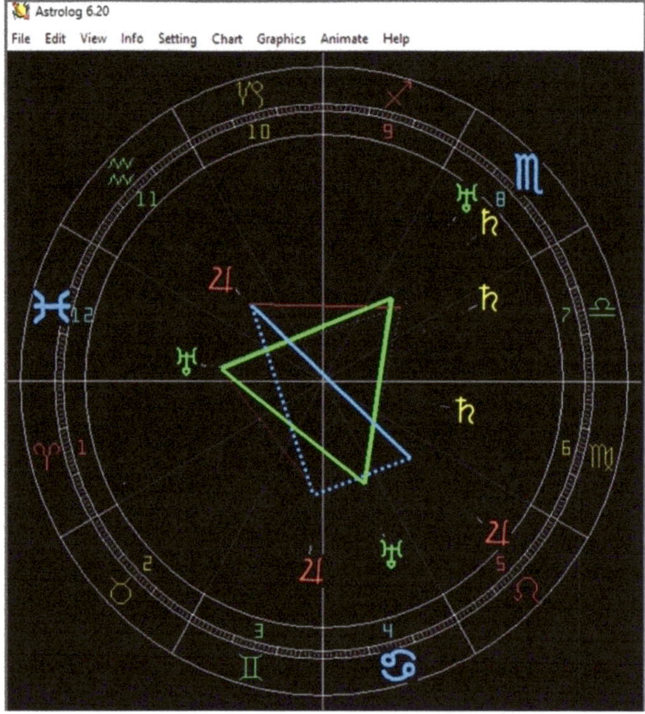

Figure 39. Comparison chart of the market lows in 1896, 1953 and 2009.

Further examining of the five market lows in Figures 38 and 39 reveals that there is no regular aspect between the positions of Jupiter. This implies that the consistent finding at these market lows is the natal trine relationship between the positions of Uranus at 23° ***after common Saturn/fire sign highs.***

To finish this analysis we now need to look at the lows after a Saturn/Aries market top. This analysis is critical for the timing of next market low which will occur in the late 2020's. Figure 40 shows the lows of 1914 and 1970 which were both after the Saturn/Aries highs of 1909 and 1968. The 1914 low is problematic as there is a gap in the DJI due to the market closure from July to December because of the first world-war. Nevertheless, using the slightly earlier date of November 1914, you can see a similar trine relationship between the positions of Uranus and this time they are in the ***air signs*** of Libra and Aquarius.

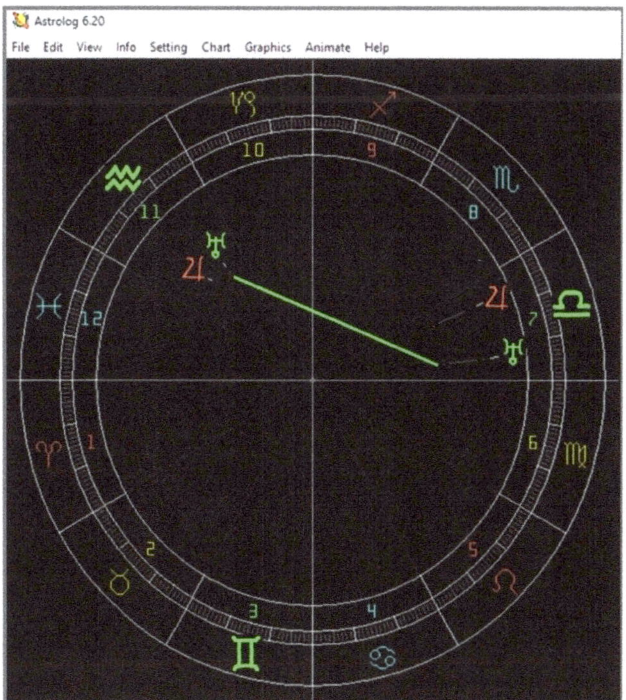

Figure 40. Comparison chart of the market lows in 1914 and 1970 showing a trine aspect.

You can also see that, at these two market lows, Uranus is not at 23°. In this case Uranus appears to be at 7° within the air signs. Now you might think this finding has ruined the Uranus/market low hypothesis, but before we throw out this idea there a a few things to consider. Firstly, the approach of analysing the groups of lows after each of the Sagitarius/Leo/Aries highs appears to be justified as each of these groups of market lows are in different zodiac elements. The lows within each group all seem to share the same natal aspect (trine), but the element (fire, water or air) in which the Uranus/ market low occurs appears to be dependent on the fire sign of the market high. Saturn/Sagitarius highs are followed by Uranus/market lows in ***fire signs***, Saturn/Leo highs are followed by lows in ***water signs*** and the Saturn/Aries highs are followed by lows in ***air signs***.

A second thing to consider is the angular relationship between 7° and 23° within a (30°) zodiac sign. 7° is simply 7° from the start of the sign. 23° is the mirror image of this at 7° from the end of the sign. So as you can see, there is a symmetry between these angles suggesting the 7° trine pattern may still be legitimate.

We have already seen the natal Uranus trine pattern in each of the three water signs after Leo highs (Figure 39). To prove the existance of similar natal trine patterns in the fire and air signs, it is worthwhile working backwards through previous cycles using the years in the original K rows of Gann's financial timetable (Figure 25).

The first cycle back from the inception of the DJI brings us to the years 1877-78. These years are 3-4 years after the 1873 land peak (Figure 24) and are immediately after a Saturn/Sagitarius alignment. So we ask the question "during this time was Uranus at a position to form a natal trine with the other fire sign lows?" In 1877 Uranus was at 23° Leo (for a second time) forming a perfect trine with the lows of 1932 and 1987. So this appears to consolidate the concept of (fire sign) Uranus natal trine lows following a Saturn/Saggitarius high.

The next cycle back includes the years 1859-1860, 3-4 years after the 1856 land peak. These years are after a Saturn/Aries alignment so we are looking for a 7° configuration. In the years 1859-60 there were indeed three occasions when Uranus was 7° Gemini completing a natal trine pattern with the market lows in 1914 and 1970. Thus the third, 7° trine pattern is proven in the air elements after a Saturn/Aries high.

Whilst this analytical approach is somewhat speculative due to the lack of comparable market data, it is highly suggestive of a market low/natal trine relationship with the positions of Uranus. Further to this, the element in which the natal trine is formed depends on the house in which Saturn was positioned at the previous market high.

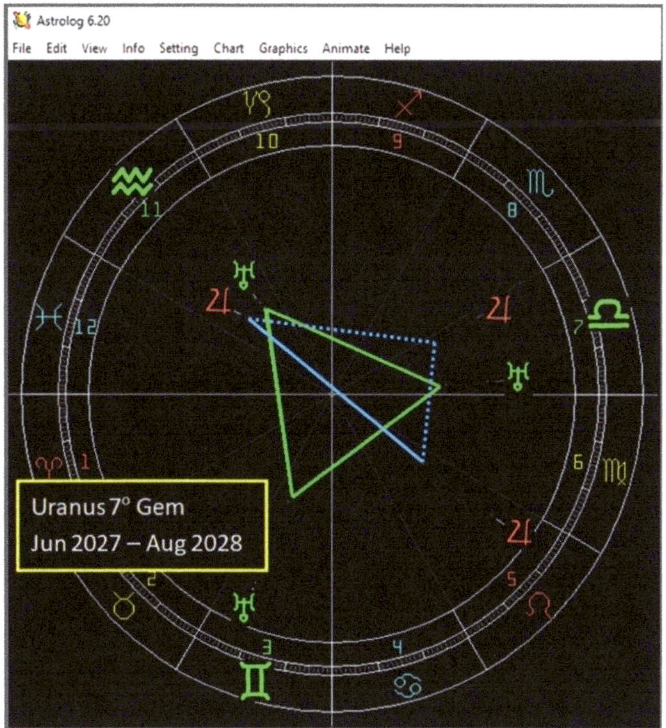

Figure 41. The natal Uranus air sign trine between the market lows of 1914, 1970 and June 2027.

The all important next market high in 2026-27 will be a Saturn/ Aries high and so, based on our findings in this section, we would expect a Uranus/air sign low. Geocentric Uranus will oscillate through 7° Gemini from June 2027 until April 2028. This includes the significant dates of two solstices and two equinoxes. Figure 41 below shows the natal Uranus trine (with the lows in 1914 and 1970) which will occur in June 2027 (outer ring).

Adding this new information into Gann's financial timetable, Figure 42 shows the Saturn/DJI market highs and the Uranus lows as discussed above. Uranus is the slowest of the three planets and although its heliocentric movement is only about three months per degree, its geocentric movement is much longer. Geocentric Uranus can spend between 10-18 months oscillating across one degree of the zodiac depending on the number of retrograde movements. It is this broader time window of geocentric Uranus that is used here together with heliocentric Saturn for the market tops. Notice the close alignment of the Uranus lows with Gann's original "K" rows. But more critically, notice that all the Uranus low time periods are vertically separate from the Saturn/fire sign time periods except for 1987. In 1987 you can see an overlap in the vertical red line (market top) and black line (market bottom). This implies that the

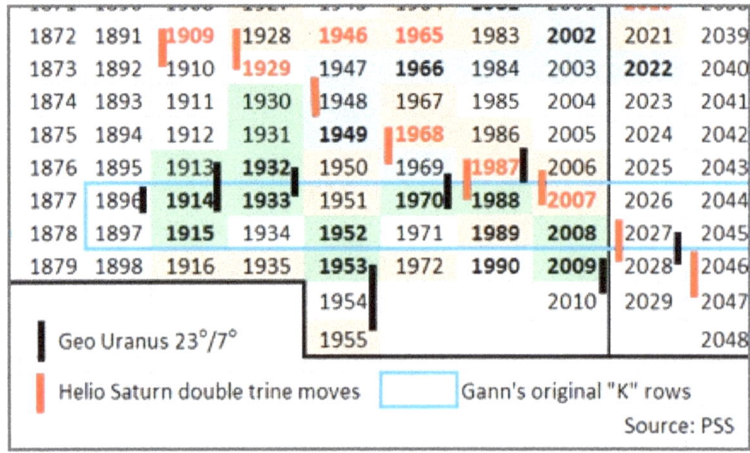

1872	1891	1909	1928	1946	1965	1983	2002	2021	2039
1873	1892	1910	1929	1947	1966	1984	2003	2022	2040
1874	1893	1911	1930	1948	1967	1985	2004	2023	2041
1875	1894	1912	1931	1949	1968	1986	2005	2024	2042
1876	1895	1913	1932	1950	1969	1987	2006	2025	2043
1877	1896	1914	1933	1951	1970	1988	2007	2026	2044
1878	1897	1915	1934	1952	1971	1989	2008	2027	2045
1879	1898	1916	1935	1953	1972	1990	2009	2028	2046
				1954			2010	2029	2047
				1955					2048

Geo Uranus 23°/7°
Helio Saturn double trine moves
Gann's original "K" rows
Source: PSS

Figure 42. Gann's financial time table showing Uranus market lows.

time from the top of the market to bottom should have been short. History tells us that the 1987 market crash was indeed very rapid (three weeks) and very violent. If you look further at Figure 42, you can see that there is another overlap of these lines in the upcoming 2027-28 time period. Whether this alignment is again significant is unknown, but importantly the position of Uranus at this time is also in accordance with Jensen's war cycle (7-9° Gemini). This will be the first time since the Civil War that the war cycle and the end of the economic cycle are aligned. With this in mind, it is of some concern to consider what may trigger a violent market collapse.

Jupiter timing

The above investigations have used two of Jensen's planets (Saturn and Uranus) to define the market tops and bottoms. His third planet (Jupiter) has not shown any consistent pattern at either the top or bottom of the market. But Jensen included Jupiter in his analysis and so we should not ignore it. As the fastest moving planet of the three, it can be used in a different way. It can be used to better time the major trend reversals by reducing the time windows defined by Saturn and Uranus. And by so doing we stumble across further insights into the planetary aspects which are alluded to by Jensen.

If we review the natal astrology Figures 32 and 33 (market tops), and Figures 38, 39 and 40 (market bottoms) it can be seen that Jupiter is in no fixed house of the zodiac, but it is often close to the highly significant 23° position within a variety of houses. To incorporate this finding into our timing analysis, we can consider adding a Jupiter 15°-30° time window (of the relevant zodiac house) as we have done with Saturn at the fire sign market tops.

Figure 43 shows the six market tops overlaid with the heliocentric Saturn/fire sign and heliocentric Jupiter 15-30° time frames. You can see how the time window is reduced when only the time that is common to ***both*** planets is considered. You should note that the

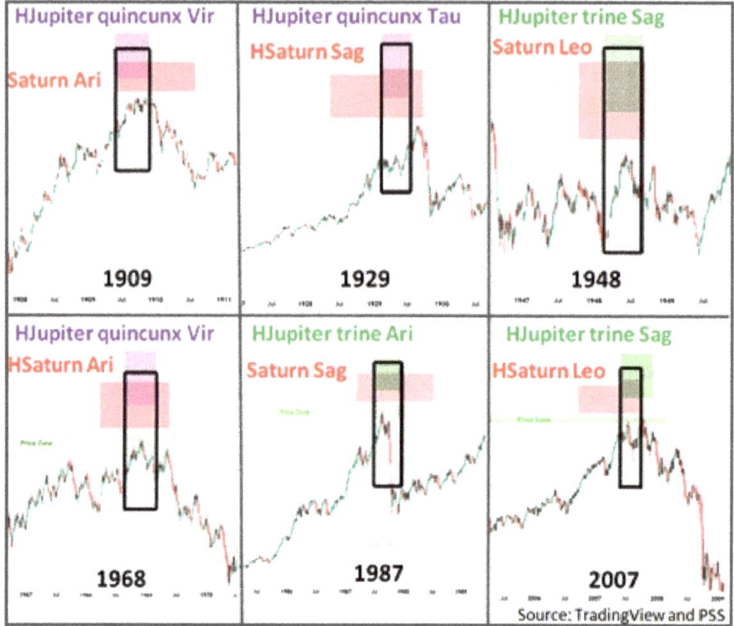

Figure 43. The six DJI market tops overlaid with the Saturn and Jupiter 15°-30° time windows.

23° time point for each of these planets is exactly in the centre of each of their time ranges as their heliocentric movement is at a constant pace across the range.

Figure 43 allows you to follow Saturn's double trine, fire sign movements from one cycle top to the next. You can also see how using the positions of both planets improves the timing of the market tops. The only possible exception is the 1929 top, but some commentators have suggested that even Gann did not expect the last exuberant market thrust into September 1929. Even so it is clear that using this approach it is possible to reduce the expected time frame for the market top down to a few months out of a nineteen to twenty year cycle.

There is a second point of interest that comes from Figure 43. And that is the analysis of the Saturn/Jupiter aspects. Jensen stated that planetary aspects were associated with both economic prosperity and depression. A trine (120°) aspect being correlated with prosperity whilst a square (90°) or opposite (180°) aspect heralded a depression. If we examine the aspects of Saturn and Jupiter for the six DJI market tops we find that three of the highs show a trine aspect whilst the other three show a quincunx (150°) aspect. This finding emphasizes the importance of only looking for the planetary aspects at the appropriate time. In this case only when Saturn is 15°-30° in a fire sign and only at every second fire sign (after a double trine movement) in concert with the market tops. It should be noted that this analysis shows that none of the market highs demonstrate a (cardinal) conjunct/square/opposite aspect at these times, supporting Jensen's hypothesis for Saturn/Jupiter aspects and prosperity.

In astrology the 120° (trine) aspect is mentioned frequently, but the 150° (quincunx or inconjunct) aspect is probably the least known of the zodiac angles. It is simply five (30°) houses of the zodiac (quin meaning 5). This aspect is not discussed much, but was well known to Gann. The planets associated with two of the main characters in TTTTA move 2670° (7 cycles plus a quincunx) over a critical time period in the book.

So if we now look at the timing and the angular movement of heliocentric Saturn and Jupiter between the market tops an interesting pattern emerges. The "standard 20 year" cycle of Saturn and Jupiter entails a total movement of 840°. Saturn has a double trine movement of 240° and Jupiter has a movement of one and two thirds cycles or 600°. Added together that makes 840° of total planetary movement. This cycle can be measured from the planetary conjunction to conjunction, but it can also be measured from market top to market top. So the timing of the market tops can be measured, not only in Earth years, but also in degrees of (Saturn/Jupiter) planetary movement.

Figure 43 shows that at the 1909 and 1929 highs the aspect of Saturn and Jupiter was the same (both show a quincunx). So the twenty years between these market tops represents the "standard" 840° total movement because the aspect is the same at both tops. However, the next (war affected) high in 1948 had a trine aspect. This indicates that

Jupiter only moved 570° in this cycle, so there was 30° less planetary movement over that 19 year period. The total planetary movement in this instance was therefore only 810°, explaining the shorter time frame. The next high in 1968 again had a quincunx aspect so the planetary movement in this 20 year cycle was 870° because this time Jupiter moved 630°, resulting in a longer cycle. As explained earlier, this variation is due to the elliptical orbits of these two planets. This sequence follows on with a shorter 19 year/810° cycle to 1987 and then a 20 year/840° cycle to 2007. Using this methodology, the current cycle is also predicted to peak after 20 years and 840° of planetary movement.

So once again we see this 19-20 year, market top cycle alluded to in the last chapter. But looking at this same market movement using planetary angular movements rather than Earth years helps to explain the slightly irregular working of this cycle. The Saturn/Jupiter cycle was undoubtedly one of Gann's master cycles. Using it in this particular way is well suited to the DJI and helps to clarify the subtle variations in the cycle of the major market tops. Understanding these variations gives you the best chance of using the cycle to your benefit.

For the market lows we need to use the positions of geocentric Uranus and geocentric Jupiter. Figure 44 shows the seven market bottoms including 1896.

Although there is no real consistency to the position of Jupiter at these lows, there are still individual patterns here. The Uranus/ fire sign lows (which occur after the Saturn/Sagittarius highs) all coincide with Jupiter in a fire sign and at a trine aspect (Figure 38). These 1932 and 1987 lows are the ones mentioned by Olga in 2010. If you review the 1877 (pre-DJI) Uranus/fire sign low (mentioned above) you will see that Jupiter at this time was in Sagittarius, again forming a perfect fire sign trine with 1932 Jupiter and 1987 Jupiter.

The other (air and water signs) Uranus lows show a different pattern for Jupiter. In the three Uranus/water sign lows (after the Saturn/Leo

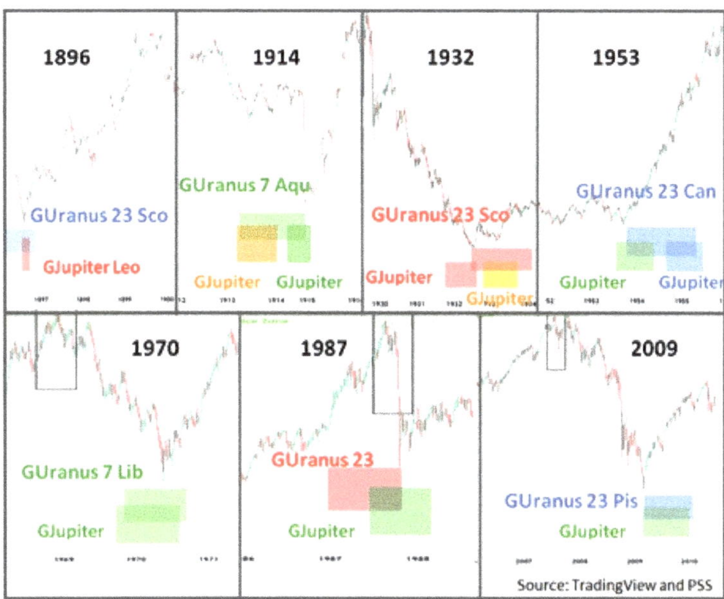

Figure 44. The seven market lows with the Uranus/Jupiter time windows.

highs) it can be seen (Figure 39) that the natal positions of Jupiter include an opposition (Aquarius and Leo) together with a third position (Gemini) which is trine/sextile (120° from one Jupiter and 60° from the other). The Uranus/air sign lows (after the Saturn/Aries highs), which include the coming 2027 alignment, show the potential for a similar pattern. Figure 41 shows a similar natal Jupiter/opposition (Aquarius and Leo) and trine/sextile (Libra) pattern for June 2027. You should note that there is a second Uranus/Jupiter overlap from late 2027, but by this time Jupiter is in Virgo and no longer in natal opposition.

Whilst the patterns of Uranus and Jupiter at the market lows are not as clear or consistent as the patterns we have seen for the market highs, there are potentially important, re-occurring alignments to be seen. These planetary aspects should be noted for future reference. The first "test" for this theory will occur in just a few years at the upcoming market low in 2027-28.

Chapter 8
Putting it all Together

In the previous chapters I have progressively introduced various concepts, ending with the land and DJI market cycles. However, when attempting to put together a market forecast, these concepts should be addressed in the reverse order. The simple time counts and the major time cycles need to be established first, so that we know ***when*** to apply the other technical details.

The US land cycle (Chapter 6) is the main, cyclic driver of the US/world's share markets. For this reason it is crucial that the current position within that cycle is established before anything else. Luckily, this is can be accomplished relatively easily by reviewing the evidence provided by our two market leading, land indicators.

Firstly, the US building permits in Figure 45 shows the last two cycles and the first twelve years of the current cycle. Some basic technical analysis in the form of support/resistance levels and trend lines has been added to provide some clarity. You can see that building permits broke downwards through significant support levels in both 1987 and 2006 prior to the DJI market tops in 1987 and 2007. The current (building permits) cycle started in 2011 and a strong up trend can be seen defined by the trend line. In late 2022 the number of building permits broke this trend line similar to early 2006. At the time of writing, permits have now made a temporary low establishing a significant support level. This is similar to the establishment of support levels in mid 1987 and late 2006. Using

2011 as the critical starting point of the current cycle, a time count of 14 years suggests the possibility of a break down through this major level in 2025.

Figure 45. US building permits showing the current cycle to 2023.

The second market leading indicator is the Case-Schiller 20-city home price index (Figure 46). Re-visiting this indicator you can see clearly the top of the last cycle in 2006 (red arrow) in concert with the building permits peak in Figure 45. The decline in land prices through the GFC was followed by a period of consolidation until the current cycle starting in 2012 (green arrow). The land/ home price then increased steadily through a recovery phase until the mid cycle slowdown/COVID crash in 2020. Note that the land price did not decline through this crisis. The mid cycle slowdown this not the same as the destructive end-of-cycle collapse (2006-2012) because the land price does not breakdown at this point. Following 2020 you can see the inflection point in the land price as the market enters the frenetic, second half of the cycle. Counting fourteen years from 2012 brings us to 2026 when another catastrophic collapse of land values is expected, heralding a severe economic downturn.

So you can see clear evidence that the current land cycle is tracking in a known, predictable manner similar to previous cycles. These charts suggest that we are about three years away

Figure 46. The Case-Shiller 20-city home price index showing the current cycle to 2023.

from a likely land cycle top. By 2026 it is expected that the building permits will have broken downwards and the land/home price graph will be turning over. This will go totally unnoticed by the rest of the market and by the economic commentators. The "land" was written out of economic teaching 100 years ago and the so-called "experts" have no concept of land history or its critical role in the economy.

Evidence of these events will be seen in price charts of the large US building companies such as DH Horton (DHI), Toll Brothers (TOL), Meritage Homes (MTH), Lennar Corporation (LEN) and PulteGroup (PMH). The share market always looks 6-12 months ahead when pricing a company's worth. As the land price tops out and the building rates decline, the profitability of these building companies will come under pressure. By 2025-26, an examination of these price charts will show that they have topped out and are now in a down trend.

If you are a property investor, these simple indicators give you the time frame on which to base buying and/or selling your properties. But this book is not property-focused. The land/real estate cycle is purely used to gauge the underlying economic cycle with a view to timing share market investment.

So now we understand the timing of the land/economic cycle, and keeping the potential 2026 cycle top at the front of our mind, we can start to overlay the two Gann cycles that are relevant to the (DJI) share market.

Firstly, the Moon's nodal cycle which is the basis for Gann's financial timetable (Figure 29). This timetable is essentially the land cycle with the timing of the Moon's node in Pisces and then Aquarius being the critical time points for the end of cycle.

Secondly, the Saturn/Jupiter cycle, with the overlap of the Saturn and Jupiter timing windows having demonstrated the previous market tops.

Figure 47 shows the DJI for the last few years out to 2029 with the annotations of these two cycles.

The Moon's node is in Pisces for most of 2025 through to August 2026 for an expected land cycle top. You can see how this timing aligns with the timing derived from the real price data in the above building permit and home price charts.

Figure 47 also shows that heliocentric Saturn is at 15°-30° Aries from January 2027 to March 2028. When adding in the Jupiter timing, you will note that there are two periods when there is coincident Jupiter 15°-30°. The first period (Jupiter in Leo) from January 2027 to May 2027, and the second (Jupiter in Virgo) from December 2027 to March 2028. Whilst both of these time frames are valid, the first (Leo) time window would seen more likely when considering the node-in-Pisces timing and the fourteen year time count for the land cycle from early 2012.

Interestingly, whilst the heliocentric Saturn/Jupiter cycle shows a time window in early 2027, this cycle has also demonstrated an alternating 19-20 year time count (Figures 35 and 37) which suggests a 2026 peak (chapter 7).

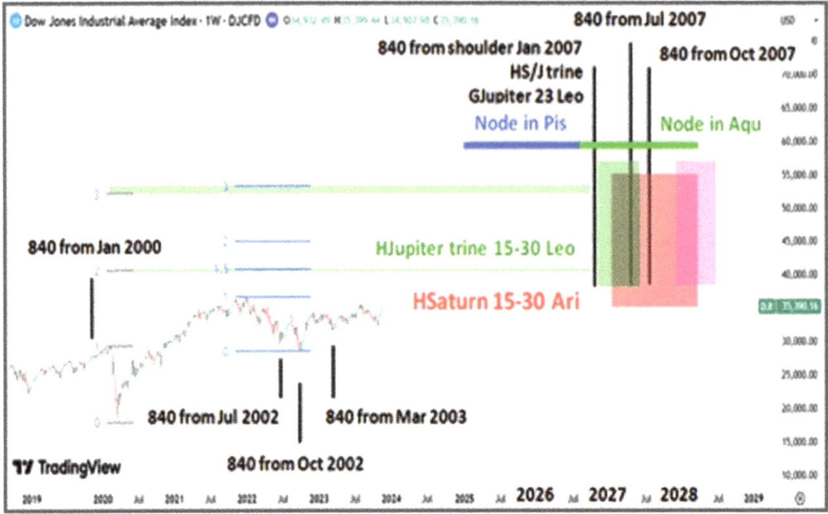

Figure 47. The current DJI chart with Gann's nodal and Saturn/ Jupiter cycles, price extensions and key points from the last cycle.

Either way, all the "big picture" evidence suggests the market will top out in 2026-27. Probably between the middle of 2026 and the middle of 2027. Having established this overall time frame, it is then possible to narrow down the potential market high by adding in three specific time points that are based on the last (2007) cycle.

A market top coincident with the Jupiter/Leo time window implies a Saturn/Jupiter trine planetary aspect, similar to the top in 2007 (Figure 43). This suggests that the current cycle is moving to a 840° Saturn/Jupiter rhythm. Figure 47 shows key turning points from the last cycle overlaid on the current cycle using an extension of 840° planetary movement (Chapter 7). You can see the close alignment of the mid-cycle high in 2020 with the extended 2000 market top, and the exact alignment of the inverted head-and-shoulders pattern from the mid-cycle low in 2002. The market peaks of July 2007 and October 2007 extend to April and July 2027. Note the coincidence of the first (840° from July 2007) peak and the Saturn/Jupiter time window, further reinforcing the relevance of this time period.

In addition, the 840° extension of the high in February 2007 is also included in this analysis. This peak was the left shoulder of the large head-and-shoulders pattern which constituted the top of the market in 2007. Its extended time point is in October 2026 which is also within the mid 2026 to mid 2027 time window. The relevance of this October 2026 time point is further reinforced by a coincident heliocentric Saturn/Jupiter trine (120°) aspect and a geocentric Jupiter 23° Leo alignment.

So using this planetary movement approach, we have ended up with three potential time points for the next market high. One within the January-May 2027 time window, and one point either side of the window.

Having established a probable ***time*** period for the market top, we can now turn our attention to the ***price*** of the market top. We can do this by overlaying the (Fibonacci) price extensions using the significant market retracements (Chapter 4). Figure 47 shows the price extensions applied to the COVID/mid cycle correction and the January/October 2022 correction. You can see that there are two potential price zones defined by the alignment of the extension levels. A very narrow zone at 41,000 is created by the nearly perfect alignment of the 2X and 1.5X extensions. Another wider zone at 53,000 is seen with the alignment of the 3X levels. Currently we have only these two retracements to work with, but there will almost certainly be at least one more significant retracement before the market top which will help differentiate these price zones.

The (Aries) market tops in 1909 and 1968 both show a pattern where the peaks were at levels the market had reached 2-3 years previously. So it is possible that the DJI may rise to 41,000 in the near future, reflect off this level and return to it in 2026-27. Alternatively, 2024 is a presidential election year and the incumbent administration will flood the economy with money in the lead up to the election. This may push the market through the 41,000 level making the 53,000 more likely.

We can only sit back and watch the market progression over the next few years. Adding in extra information as it comes to hand. Finally, as the market "shows" itself in the last year or two of the cycle, we will be able to draw our scaled Gann fans to further reinforce one or more time points at the relevant price zone (Chapter 5).

As the market peak is revealed it will be possible to consider the coming market low. We do this by drawing Gann fans and price retracement levels to define time and price points for the low (Chapter 5). The 2009 market low will certainly be one of the key reference points from which to draw these levels. The 2020 COVID low will also probably be another time/price point. Currently we cannot achieve this as we do not know where the top of the market is going to be. But whilst we wait for that to be revealed, we can add in the planetary time window using geocentric Uranus at 7° Gemini in 2027-28 as a potential time for the market bottom. Figure 48 shows the geocentric positions of Uranus/Jupiter along with the 840° (Saturn/Jupiter) extensions from the major lows in 2008-09. You will note the considerable overlap between the time windows of heliocentric Saturn (top) and geocentric Uranus (bottom). But incorporating the positions of Jupiter does allow for some time separation between the potential top and bottom of the market. You should also note that whilst the extension of the 2009 market low is well outside the Uranus time window, two of the earlier 2008 low extensions result in November 2027 and May 2028 time points, both of which are within the second critical Uranus/Jupiter overlap. Additionally, only the first extension (November 2027) is within the node-in-Aquarius window. Either way these findings are suggestive of a rapid market decline after the final top is reached and raises the possibility that both the market top and bottom could be within the 2027 year. This conclusion is quite frightening and reinforces the need to follow the market and the economy during these last frenetic years of this cycle. Taking (financial) action before the final market peak will be critical to preserving your investments. This becomes even more significant when you consider that the severity and duration of the market collapse could be exacerbated by the effects of the war cycle and the culmination of the Kondratiev cycle (Chapter 6).

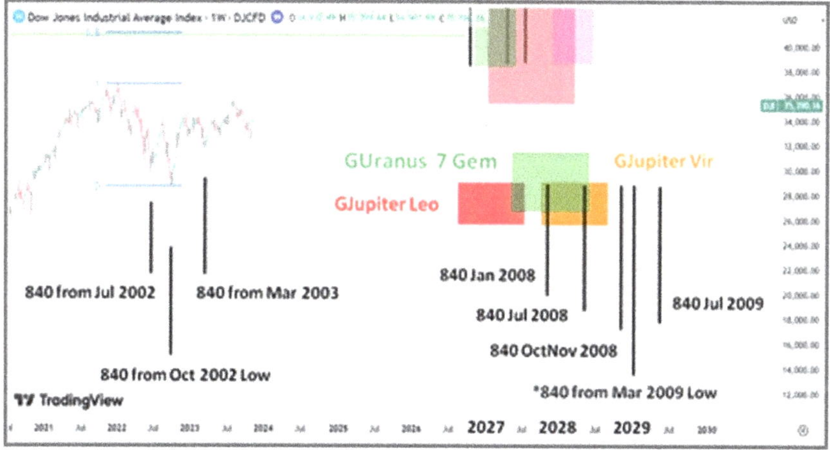

Figure 48. The DJI chart showing the Uranus 7° Gemini time window and the extended lows from 2008-09.

Chapter 9
Conclusion

If you are still reading at this point, then I congratulate you. What started out as a simple collection of my thoughts on WD Gann and his principles has ended up being quite a deep and increasingly complex dive into the study of esoteric time cycles. The study of time and the principles of Gann is truly a never ending journey. And, as I alluded to in the Preface, I have gained many insights during the compilation of this document.

In the age of computers, investors have the ability to easily access information on market fundamentals along with charting and technical analysis packages. In this book I have attempted to take the reader with these skills and extend their knowledge by adding in Gann's principles of time and time cycles. These concepts will be challenging for some people, but the notion of planetary based time cycles should not be foreign to us. If you think about it, we already (unthinkingly) use the Earthly time cycles of the daily planetary rotation and the yearly planetary revolution to track the passage of time. Gann's idea of also using other planets simply provides us with an alternative way of measuring time.

Understanding the world's economy is a major challenge when we think of it only in Earth time. The true rhythm of the economic cycle is largely hidden from us using this approach. Gann's concept of using other time cycles is one way of clarifying this rhythm. The obscure 18.6 year land cycle is more easily followed by using the single, 360° cycle of the Moon's north node. The erratic timing of the major market peaks is better predicted by using the angular movement of Saturn and Jupiter. These two cycles allow the clearest visualization of the cyclic economic rhythm. Understanding the cycle timing and your current time point within the cycle are the two most important things you can ever learn. The so called "experts" have no idea about this and consequently it is no surprise that they get their forecasts so wrong. The periodic, rhythmic economic "busts" are not "black swan events". They are the violent end of each cycle and are entirely predictable.

Regular economic collapses have been happening for hundreds of years. Over one hundred years ago the American economist Henry George recognised that land price was the main driver of the boom/bust economic cycle. He proposed a solution to this endless cycle with specific land tax reform. These changes are well known to the "Georgists" throughout the world. Unfortunately the (property based) "establishment" has selfishly suppressed the role of the "land" and this tax change has never been implemented. The result is that these boom/bust economic cycles are set to continue.

The end-of-cycle economic collapse affects everyone. Your finances, businesses, employment and relationships all suffer through these low periods. It is hard to avoid being affected to some degree. But by understanding the cycle and the timing of the cycle there is the opportunity to take mitigating action to avoid the worst effects.

Making the right decision at the right time can change your life, but you have to take action. Taking action is difficult. Having the confidence to move your investments at a time when the markets are booming is very challenging. In the age of the internet, moving retirement funds only requires a simple click of a computer mouse. But it is still incredibly difficult. Making property, business or employment adjustments are even harder.

I am always aided in this process by the famous quote attributed to Warren Buffett. "Be fearful when others are greedy and be greedy only when others are fearful". This contrarian approach to investment has been enormously successful for him and it fits exactly with an understanding of the time cycles.

In addition to acknowledging the hidden time points within the economic cycle we have also discussed the hidden price points in the DJI. Knowing the critical time points of the market allows the timely application of the enhanced technical tools. It is possible to "zoom in" and estimate the highs/lows of the market using the Fibonacci price extension tool and the Gann fan. These tools, calibrated with specific numbers and ratios that are found repeatedly in Gann's work, allow an accurate indication of the market's major turning points.

After analysing the first six DJI market cycles I have extrapolated the findings to predict the top of the next market cycle in 2026-27. The accuracy of that prediction will be judged in time, but perhaps the more important "take home" message here is to understand the cyclic, predictable nature of these economic events. The US land market and the US share market are going to peak in the near future. The subsequent economic collapse is likely to be rapid, severe and exacerbated by world events. You need to be ready.

The confidence to take action comes slowly, but with increased understanding of Gann's cycles, the opportunities become clear. Most of us will never acquire Gann's level of understanding, but the knowledge in this book is sufficient to make a significant difference to your financial future.

In this book I have attempted to expand your understanding of the economic cycles by showing evidence of Gann's time principles in the DJI over the last 130 years. However this book is not just about economics or investment. It is about hope. Hope that by better understanding the basis of the boom/bust cycles, you can track the turning of the cycle and make a difference to your future.

In many ways we are no different to the Celts who 5,000 years ago stood in Stonehenge and watched the late December sunrise. For them, tracking the movement of the sun proved the turning of seasonal cycle which, in a link across the millennia, also provided hope for better times.

Whether this book is your first step into WD Gann's esoteric world of time travel or just another step along the way, I wish you well on your journey.

The Doctor
Adelaide, South Australia
December 2023.

About the Author

Dr Peter Sutton-Smith was born in Adelaide, South Australia. In 1975 he graduated from Flinders University with an honours degree in biological Science. He completed his PhD at Adelaide University in the late 1980's. He was employed as a medical scientist to run medical pathology laboratories which focused on renal (kidney) disease and renal transplantation. This work included involvement with research programs and a teaching role as a higher degree supervisor for post graduate students.

He brought this same analytical approach to share market investment. Investing started in the conventional way with financial advisors and managed funds, but this was replaced with self management after experiencing the inflexibility of this approach during the 2002 market downturn. He preferred to make his own investment decisions rather than have a third party involved.

For over twenty years he has traded the markets and used the hard won lessons to evolve the management of his retirement account. During the last 15 years he has increasingly incorporated the time principles of DW Gann into his investment decisions.

Peter still lives in Adelaide with his wife. They are now comfortably retired on the proceeds of their superannuation which has been greatly enhanced by the knowledge contained in this book.

www.ingramcontent.com/pod-product-compliance
Lightning Source LLC
LaVergne TN
LVHW052354100826
845147LV00013B/838

* 9 7 8 0 6 4 6 7 3 8 9 8 7 *